Tried and Tested Primary Science Experiments

The modern world needs more scientists and engineers, and good science education is key to filling this gap. Especially in the current climate of rapid curriculum changes, a lack of emphasis on training can result in unconfident teaching and monotonous lessons. To rectify this, this book offers methods to deliver the National Curriculum aims at primary school in an interesting, hands-on and fun fashion.

Tried and Tested Primary Science Experiments provides a practical step-by-step guide for all year groups, helping teachers to create more engaging and fun science lessons in the classroom. All experiments are simple to follow, fail-safe and are designed to enthuse and inspire students. It includes:

- tried and tested guides to running successful science experiments;
- clear instructions that outline the simple equipment required, how to carry out the experiments and what results to expect;
- suggestions for adapting each activity to the special needs and interests of the students.

Aimed at primary school teachers and trainee teachers, this illustrated guide refers directly to the new curriculum and is an essential resource for every primary classroom.

Kirsty Bertenshaw is an award-winning science teacher and is founder and director of STEMtastic education consultancy. She is a regular columnist for *Education Today* and has also delivered a training session for the Science Learning Centre in York.

Tried and Tested Primary Science Experiments

Practical Enhancements for Science in the Primary Curriculum

Kirsty Bertenshaw

Routledge
Taylor & Francis Group

LONDON AND NEW YORK

First published 2019
by Routledge
2 Park Square, Milton Park, Abingdon, Oxon OX14 4RN

and by Routledge
52 Vanderbilt Avenue, New York, NY 10017

Routledge is an imprint of the Taylor & Francis Group, an informa business

British Library Cataloguing-in-Publication Data
A catalogue record for this book is available from the British Library

Library of Congress Cataloging-in-Publication Data
Names: Bertenshaw, Kirsty, author.
Title: Tried and tested primary science experiments : practical enhancements for science in the primary curriculum / Kirsty Bertenshaw.
Description: Abingdon, Oxon ; New York, NY : Routledge, 2019. | Includes index.
Identifiers: LCCN 2019003041 (print) | LCCN 2019009890 (ebook) | ISBN 9780429454936 (eb) | ISBN 9781138317819 (hbk) | ISBN 9781138317826 (pbk) | ISBN 9780429454936 (ebk)
Subjects: LCSH: Science–Study and teaching (Primary) | Science–Experiments. | Science projects.
Classification: LCC LB1532 (ebook) | LCC LB1532 .B47 2019 (print) | DDC 372.35/044–dc23
LC record available at https://lccn.loc.gov/2019003041

ISBN: 978-1-138-31781-9 (hbk)
ISBN: 978-1-138-31782-6 (pbk)
ISBN: 978-0-429-45493-6 (ebk)

Typeset in Helvetica
by Wearset Ltd, Boldon, Tyne and Wear

Printed and bound in Great Britain by
TJ International Ltd, Padstow, Cornwall

Contents

Preface

Tried and Tested Primary Science Experiments aims to be a guide for primary teachers wishing to enhance their science teaching. We all know science is an important subject in schools, and that we are not producing enough scientists and engineers for the modern world. Enthusiasm comes from good experiences at an early age. This book offers methods to deliver the National Curriculum aims at primary school in an interesting, practical and fun fashion. The sparse aims of the National Curriculum and the lack of emphasis or training in science subjects can lead to unconfident teaching and monotonous lessons. This guide will show all teachers how to include practical science in primary teaching, with easy to replicate practical ideas that do not require specialist equipment or labs, but can, in most cases, be found in the store cupboard or supermarket.

Unlike other resources, this guide focuses on the learning objective and gives an activity to deliver the learning, as opposed to an activity and how it relates to the curriculum. This ensures that each practical has a purpose and the learning takes priority. Practical ideas are given for each year of primary school, and each topic of science from the National Curriculum. As the National Curriculum follows a spiral pattern, each year group revisits a topic area, building on previous knowledge and developing new understanding. The practical ideas are designed to meet the statutory and, where possible, non-statutory requirements to ensure a complete teaching and learning experience.

Sometimes a topic area cannot be explored using traditional experiments, so alternative methods such as card games are described to ensure some form of practical in every lesson!

Each practical guide is written in a step-by-step format which can be adapted to each class's needs, differentiating the activity as appropriate or even stimulating imagination in teachers to develop their own methods for teaching the content. After all, the classroom teacher knows the student's needs.

Year 1 Plants

GROWING PLANTS

Equipment:
Cress seeds
Fast growing flower seeds – sunflower, marigold, nasturtium
Cotton wool
Soil
Plant pots
Petri dishes or small plastic containers

Instructions:
1. Place cotton wool into a Petri dish or small plastic container.
2. Add enough water to soak the cotton wool without it sitting in a puddle.
3. Place a generous amount of cress seeds onto the cotton wool and place on a windowsill.
4. Observe daily.
5. Fill a small plant pot with soil.
6. Place a few flower seeds in each pot and water regularly.
7. Observe weekly – these should germinate in approximately 14 days.

The cress will grow quickly and allows students to observe germination, seeing the roots grow and the shoots sprout to become a stem. The cress can then be compared to the slower growing flowering plants, identifying common features of plants.

The growth stages can be sketched by the students or changes recorded using photography and turned into a display, including seed production in sunflowers.

Health and safety

Hazard and risk	Precautions
Seeds can pose a choking hazard and can be toxic.	Use under supervision. Do not allow students to ingest seeds.
Plastic pots, Petri dishes and plant pots can break and cause cuts.	Check for chips and damage before using. Discard any damaged objects.
Soil can contain microbes and parasites.	Adult supervision required, hands must be washed well with soap after activity. Do not allow students to ingest soil.
Cotton wool is a suffocation and choking hazard.	Adult supervision required, do not allow students to place cotton wool over their faces or ingest it.
Water spillages can be a slipping hazard.	Clear any spilt water immediately.

Adapting the activity
Extra support: give students labels such as 'shoot', 'stem', 'leaf' and a large diagram of the plant growing. Students can stick the labels onto the right part of the diagram.
Extension: replant the seeds from the flowers grown and repeat the observations.
Optional extras: recognise simple differences between flowering plants and non-flowering plants, e.g. flowers produce seeds.

SEASONS

Equipment:
A view of outside
Pencils
Paper
Camera
A school year

Instructions:
Observe a view of outside the classroom, possibly of the school field, ensuring a view of deciduous trees.

Students can observe and sketch the tree in all seasons, or take a photograph, starting with the turning of the leaves in autumn. These observations can be repeated each season. Over time, the observations can be assembled into a display. One option is to make a display of a tree with a trunk and bare branches, where students can add to a quarter of it for each season, e.g. large leaves for summer, small leaves for spring and possibly blossom, no leaves for winter and multicoloured leaves sparsely arranged for autumn.

Adapting the activity
Extra support: provide the children with pictures of a scene from every season to compare the differences in the plants.
Extension: predict the changes in the trees for each season.
Optional extras: provide the children with pictures of a scene from every season that includes evergreen trees too.

CLASSIFICATION OF TREES

Equipment:
Classification keys
Leaf samples
An outside area with access to plants and trees

Instructions:
Version 1
Using classification keys, explore the outside area and identify common garden and wild plants, and trees.

Version 2
Using a sheet with pictures of common plants in the school area pre-prepared by staff, students can tick off the ones they find in the area, or even make a tally of how many they find.

Version 3
Students can collect leaves from a variety of plants and produce their own classification key of common plants found in the school area, with the aid of staff.

Health and safety

Hazard and risk	Precautions
Plants can contain toxins, thorns or spikes.	Adult supervision required.
Allergies to plants and insect bites.	Check allergies of students before commencing activity. Be aware of insect activity in the school area – avoid areas near any biting or stinging insect nests.

Adapting the activity
Extra support: introduce students to common plants in the school area by going around as a small group and naming them.

Extension: produce a classification key that can be swapped with other students.

Optional extras: take a trip to a local park and identify species of plants there.

DECIDUOUS AND EVERGREEN

Equipment:
Small branches from evergreen trees and deciduous trees
Magnifying glasses
Thin paper
Crayons or chalk

Instructions:
Examine the small branches from both deciduous trees and evergreen trees. Use magnifying glasses to see the details clearly.

Place a leaf under a thin piece of paper. Using a crayon or chalk on its side, rub over the leaf to leave a print of the shape and texture.

Health and safety

Hazard and risk	Precautions
Plants can contain toxins, thorns or spikes.	Adult supervision required.
Allergies to plants and insect bites.	Check allergies of students before commencing activity. Be aware of insect activity in the school area – avoid areas near any biting or stinging insect nests.
Crayons or chalk may be ingested.	Use under supervision, use non-toxic crayons and chalk.

Adapting the activity

Extra support: demonstrate the technique to students using large crayons or chalks.

Extension: produce a classification key using the leaf rubbings.

Optional extras: compare leaf shapes from different trees.

Year 1 Animals including humans

National Curriculum Statements:

*   identify and name a variety of common animals including fish, amphibians, reptiles, birds and mammals;
*   identify and name a variety of common animals that are carnivores, herbivores and omnivores;
*   describe and compare the structure of a variety of common animals (fish, amphibians, reptiles, birds and mammals, including pets);
*   identify, name, draw and label the basic parts of the human body and say which part of the body is associated with each sense.

Working scientifically:

*   identifying and classifying;
*   using their observations and ideas to suggest answers to questions.

NC Assessment Indicators

Emerging: begin to identify common animals by name, and group them as fish, amphibians, reptiles, birds and mammals.

Expected: identify common animals by name, identify which ones are carnivore, herbivore or omnivore. Describe differences between common animals.

Exceeding: describe common animals as herbivores, carnivores or omnivores. Compare the structure of common animals.

Although this area is difficult to teach in a practical way, and does not involve experiments, it can be taught in a fun and active way by using card sorts or plastic animals.

IDENTIFYING COMMON ANIMALS

Equipment:
Plastic animal models including fish, reptiles, amphibians, birds, mammals
Pictures of animals with their names on the back

Instructions:
1. In groups, give pupils an assortment of plastic animals. How could they sort them?
2. Ask pupils to identify the birds from the assortment.
3. Repeat for fish, reptiles, amphibians and mammals.
4. Ask pupils what the differences are between birds and fish. Repeat for the other groupings so pupils can identify the common features of each group.
5. Now swap to the picture cards. Ask pupils to identify which animals are which. Answers can be checked on the back of cards!

Health and safety

Hazard and risk	Precautions
Plastic animals are a choking hazard.	Adult supervision required. Avoid students placing the plastic animals in their mouths.

Adapting the activity
Extra support: introduce the names of groups to students using one example, e.g. show them a fish.

Extension: include trickier animals such as dolphins which look like fish but are mammals.

Optional extras: students can produce a poster for each vertebrate group highlighting the features of that group.

Year 1 Materials

National Curriculum Statements:

- identify and name a variety of everyday materials, including wood, plastic, glass, metal, water and rock;
- describe the simple physical properties of a variety of everyday materials;
- compare and group together a variety of everyday materials on the basis of their simple physical properties.

Working scientifically:

- gathering and recording data to help in answering questions;
- performing simple tests;
- identifying and classifying.

NC Assessment Indicators

Emerging: begin to identify everyday materials. Group together objects made from the same materials.

Expected: describe simple properties of materials and record them in a results table.

Exceeding: group together everyday materials with similar physical properties. Suggest which materials may have similar physical properties before the completion of testing.

These activities can be completed separately and combined or as a continuous exploration of science. Multiple sets of materials will be required and pupils can suggest their own properties for testing. Materials can be adjusted for each group or depending on resources available. Pupils may begin to suggest properties based on prior knowledge or apply gained knowledge to materials they are presented with. Results can be recorded in large results tables and represented as Venn diagrams, pictograms or bar charts. The grouping activity can be revisited after the physical tests have been carried out, and pupils can change their original ideas using gained knowledge.

GROUPING MATERIALS

Equipment:
Plastic boxes/trays/drawers to place sets of materials in
Plastic straw
Plastic spoon
Metal spoon
Plastic bead
Paper clip
Pencil
Wooden craft stick
Material/string lengths
Cardboard
Glass bead
Rubber eraser
Rock or pebble
Any extra party bag style objects such as bouncy balls
Optional: ice cube, water, milk – in containers with lids

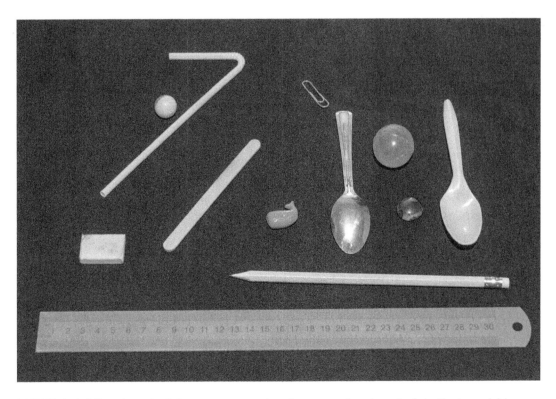

Figure 1.1 Mixed materials – an example of some mixed materials that could be chosen for this activity, but others can be added or substituted

Instructions:
1. Ask pupils to sort the materials into groups of their choice.
2. Ask pupils to justify their choices in any way, e.g. all the blue ones together, all the toys together, etc.
3. Ask pupils to identify all the objects made of wood. How do they decide which ones are made of wood?
4. Repeat for metals, plastics, glass and rubber. Question how they know which are made of that material.

Hints may be required: which ones feel cold? Which ones are shiny? Rubber can be squashed – which ones can be squashed?

Health and safety

Hazard and risk	Precautions
Rubber objects or latex bouncy balls – allergies to touching rubber or latex.	Check allergies of pupils before commencing activity. If itching or swelling occurs, stop usage of items.
Wooden objects can snap and cause splinters.	Adult supervision required. Check for chips and damage before using. Discard any snapped wooden objects.
Glass beads can smash.	Adult supervision required as beads can be dropped and broken. Check for chips and damage before using.
Metal spoon and paper clip – metal fatigue and snapping, sharp edges.	Adult supervision required as metal can wear and snap. Check for chips and damage before using. Discard any damaged spoons or paper clips.
Water or liquid spillages can be a slipping hazard. Contamination and allergy risk.	Clean up any water spillages immediately to prevent slipping hazards. Ensure liquids are not ingested. Check allergies of pupils before commencing activity.

Adapting the activity
Extra support: use hints to establish how we recognise the material, e.g. is it shiny and silvery?
Extension: include composite materials/composite, e.g. cutlery with wooden handles but metal blades, novelty pencils with plastic parts and wooden stick.
Optional extras: how would you explain how you recognise metal to an alien? Or how you recognise wood?

TESTING MATERIALS

Equipment:
Use the same objects as the sorting experiment
Cheaper metal teaspoons will bend, thicker metal spoons will not bend

Instructions:
Take each material in turn and carry out the following tests. Results can be recorded in a tick table.

Object	Bendy	See-through	Hard	Soft	Shiny	Smooth	Rough

1. Try bending the material with your hands. Does it bend? If it does, tick the box. If it does not bend, or if it breaks, draw a cross in the box.
2. Hold the object up to the light or a window. Can you see anything through the object? If you can see shadows, objects or people, tick the box. If you cannot see anything through the object, cross the box.
3. Feel the object. Squeeze it gently, then harder. Does it feel hard or soft? Tick the box for ether hard or soft.
4. Look at the object. Hold it in the light. Is it shiny? If it is shiny, tick the box.
5. Run your finger over the top of the object. Is it smooth or rough? Use the comparison that the carpet is rough but the whiteboard is smooth. Pupils may need to touch both the carpet and the whiteboard to compare surfaces. If a surface is smooth, then tick the box for smooth. If it is rough, cross the box for smooth and tick the box for rough.

Health and safety

Hazard and risk	Precautions
Rubber objects or latex bouncy balls – allergies to touching rubber or latex.	Check allergies of pupils before commencing activity. If itching or swelling occurs, stop usage of items.
Wooden objects can snap and cause splinters.	Adult supervision required . Check for chips and damage before using. Discard any snapped wooden objects.
Glass beads can smash.	Adult supervision required as beads can be dropped and broken. Check for chips and damage before using.
Metal spoon and paper clip – metal fatigue and snapping, sharp edges.	Adult supervision required as metal can wear and snap. Check for chips and damage before using. Discard any damaged spoons or paper clips.

Adapting the activity

Extra support: demonstrate each property for pupils first, e.g. bending a plastic straw. Pupils who have sensory processing issues may require longer, or to be in smaller groups for this activity.

Extension: include terminology such as waterproof, magnetic (knowledge on magnets is not required until Year 3 but some students may be familiar with the term already). Carry out tests dropping water on objects to determine if they are waterproof or absorbent.

Optional extras: explorative questioning such as 'what is made of wood in the classroom?' 'why isn't the table soft?'.

Year 1 Seasonal changes

This will be a long-term activity to measure changes in seasons and make observations, e.g. when is it most windy? What other weather do you observe on these days?

These complete measurements can be combined together along with length of day as comprehensive evidence of season changes, or used individually as appropriate. Day length information can be provided for pupils as measuring it during school time is not possible.

Pupils can conclude what changes occur at each change of season and suggest which season has the most rain, snow, wind, etc. from their results. The data may need to be displayed alongside each other to make it easier for pupils to consider it all together. Individual graphs can be drawn, or a large display graph constructed which can be added to each week.

MAKING A WIND METER

Equipment:
Two straws
Four plastic cups
Pencil with eraser or wooden dowel
Drawing pin
Hole punch

Instructions:
1. Use the hole punch to punch a hole in the side of each plastic cup, about 1–2 cm below the rim, or as far away as the hole punch will reach.
2. Hold the cup on its side, and then poke one end of the straw through the hole in the cup. Do the same to the other side of the straw, then repeat with the other two cups and straw. Make sure the cups are all facing the same direction, so they follow round in a circle. Secure to the straws with hot glue.
3. Hold the straws over each other in an X shape and then push the pin through the straws and in to the wooden dowel, or pencil eraser. The straws may need reinforcing to remain in an X shape, using hot glue

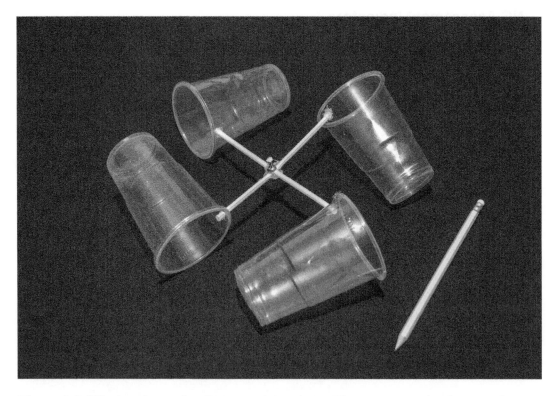

Figure 1.2 Wind meter – glue the cups into place. Please reuse plastic cups from previous uses and disassemble to recycle afterwards. Plastic straws are used as they are flexible while still maintaining their shape, and very light. Again, these can be reused

where the straws cross over. Store the wind meter in two pieces, by pulling the drawing pin out of the pencil eraser. This will prevent the wind meter from bending.

4. Make sure the cups spin freely in the wind, and then mark one of the cups with felt tips, so you can count how many revolutions per minute the wind meter makes.

5. Measure this at the same time each day and record how many revolutions per minute the wind meter makes.

Health and safety

Hazard and risk	Precautions
Weather conditions.	Wear appropriate clothing when taking measurements outside – rain coats, etc.
Drawing pins and hole punches – risk of puncturing fingers.	Supervision, staff operate hole punch and drawing pins.
Pencils or wooden stick can splinter and be sharp.	Ensure there are no sharp edges. Discard and replace stick or pencil if damaged.
Hot glue gun can cause burns.	Adults should operate the hot glue gun to lessen the risk of burning. Cool melt glue guns can be used which operate at a lower temperature.

Adapting the activity

Extra support: paint one of the cups a bright colour to aid counting.

Extension: pupils can measure at different time of day and record the results, e.g. morning, lunchtime and afternoon.

Optional extras: are there areas of the school that feel windier than others? Test the suggestions! Try angling the cups to help the wind push the cups around.

MAKING A BAROMETER

Equipment:

Clean, large glass jars
Large balloon – biodegradable balloons are preferable
Elastic bands
Straw
Sticky tape OR hot glue
Card
Pens

Instructions:

1. Cut up the balloon and stretch a piece over the open jar. Secure it with elastic bands and make sure there is no air leaking out of the jar.
2. Stick a straw with one end on the centre of the piece of balloon and the other end sticking out over the edge of the jar, using sticky tape or hot glue.
3. Now place a piece of card behind the jar – this will be how you measure changes in pressure by measuring the rise and fall of the straw. Label 'high' at the top of the paper and 'low' further down the paper to remind you what the straw movement means. Lines could be placed in between for measuring, with exactly horizontal as zero, then graduations of +1, +2 above and –1, –2 below, etc.

If the air pressure is low, the air in the jar will push up on the piece of balloon and the straw will point down – this is usually associated with a higher chance of rain or snow.

If the air pressure is high, the air will push down more on the piece of balloon causing the tip to point up – this usually indicates fair weather.

Figure 1.3 Barometer – photo taken on a rainy day, so the barometer shows as 'LOW'. Markings can be added as a standard unit, e.g. +1, +2, –1, –2 or simply record low or high pressure

Figure 1.4 Barometer top view – the straw must be stuck as close to the centre of the balloon as possible. The longer the length of straw the easier it is to read off the scale

Health and safety

Hazard and risk	*Precautions*
Weather conditions.	Wear appropriate clothing when taking measurements outside – rain coats, etc.
Glass jars can smash.	Adult supervision required as jar can be dropped and broken. Could use stiff, clear plastic cup instead.
Balloon and elastic bands – small pieces of balloon and elastic bands can be swallowed.	Count out elastic bands, do not leave unsupervised. Place waste pieces of balloon in the bin immediately.
Hot glue gun can cause burns.	Adults should operate the hot glue gun to lessen the risk of burning. Cool melt glue guns can be used which operate at a lower temperature.

Adapting the activity

Extra support: assist students in producing a barometer.

Extension: pupils might suggest links between weather and pressure.

Optional extras: keep a record of weather conditions and season alongside the record of pressure.

MEASURING RAIN WITH A RAIN GAUGE

Equipment:
Rain gauge OR plastic cup
Measuring cylinder

Instructions:
Each day, measure the amount of rain water collected in the rain gauge or plastic cup. If using a plastic cup, pour the water collected into a measuring cylinder to measure the amount of rain water collected. Record the amount and then empty it out, ready for collecting rain the next day.

Alternatively, measure out $1\,cm^3$ of water using a measuring cylinder, pour it in to the cup. Use a permanent marker to mark the water level on the cup and label it as $1\,cm^3$. Repeat this for $2\,cm^3$, $3\,cm^3$, $4\,cm^3$, $5\,cm^3$ and $6\,cm^3$. Students should now be able to read of the water level as they collect the rain gauge, rather than needing to bring in the rain gauge to measure the amount of water.

This activity is ideal for plotting a bar chart – a large bar chart on the wall could be a working display!

Health and safety

Hazard and risk	Precautions
Weather conditions.	Wear appropriate clothing when taking measurements outside – rain coats, etc.
Rain gauge, plastic cup and measuring cylinders can all shatter and cause cuts.	Adult supervision required. Discard and replace if damaged.

Adapting the activity

Extra support: provide pictures or photos of different seasons to stimulate discussion on what weather is, and what could be measured.

Extension: pupils suggest what kind of weather we could measure and record. Record morning and afternoon and compare the differences.

Optional extras: what if we consider seasonal changes in tropical zones – what happens to show changes of seasons in other places? Why is there more wind on the coast than in the middle of the country? What is a rainy season?

Year 2 Living things and their habitats

National Curriculum Statements:

- explore and compare the differences between things that are living, dead and things that have never been alive;
- identify that most living things live in habitats to which they are suited and describe how different habitats provide for the basic needs of different kinds of animals and plants, and how they depend on each other;
- identify and name a variety of plants and animals in their habitats, including micro-habitats;
- describe how animals obtain their food from plants and other animals, using the idea of a simple food chain, and identify and name different sources of food.

Working scientifically:

- identifying and classifying;
- using their observations and ideas to suggest answers to questions.

NC Assessment Indicators

Emerging: begin to identify plants and animals in their habitats.
Expected: describe how animals obtain their food in simple food chains.
Exceeding: explain that living things depend on each other in their habitats for food.

LIVING, DEAD OR NEVER ALIVE

Equipment:
Plastic boxes/trays/drawers to place sets of materials in
Plastic spoon
Metal spoon
Wooden spoon

Paper clip

Pencil

Wooden craft stick

Material/wool/cotton string lengths

Cardboard

Glass bead

Rubber eraser

Rock or pebble

Green leaf

Conker or acorn, alternatively onion or garlic bulb – check allergies first

Instructions:

1. Ask pupils to identify which objects are alive.
2. Ask pupils to identify which items were alive – were made from living things, e.g. trees.
3. Ask pupils to identify which items were never alive, e.g. rocks.
4. Pose the question: 'how do you know the wooden spoon was once alive?' to stimulate discussion.

Hints may be required: are rocks alive? Is plastic alive? Is the conker or onion alive? Will it grow if you plant it?

Health and safety

Hazard and risk	Precautions
Glass beads can smash.	Adult supervision required. Beads are less likely to have sharp edges or be easily broken. Discard if damaged.
Wooden items can snap and cause splinters.	Adult supervision required. Check items for damage and discard any items with visible splinters.
Metal spoons can snap through metal fatigue.	Cheaper metal spoons are likely to snap sooner than thicker, more expensive spoons. Check for signs of fatigue and discard if they snap or sharp edges are visible.
Allergies to seeds, rubber, wool.	Discard any dirty materials. Cereal boxes, etc. need to be in good condition and clean for use in the classroom.
Rocks or pebbles can have sharp edges causing cuts, or cause crush injuries though dropping.	Use small pieces of rock or pebbles, discard any with sharp edges, adult supervision required.

Adapting the activity

Extra support: ask students to decide where each object comes from, e.g. wooden craft sticks are from trees.

Extension: more materials can be added, and more characteristics explored such as shiny or smooth.

Optional extras: explorative questioning such as 'why is an onion still alive but a wooden craft stick is not, when they both come from plants?'

LIVING THINGS AND THEIR HABITATS

Equipment:
Thick card
Cereal boxes/small parcel boxes/shoe boxes
Plasticine or modelling clay
Pipe cleaners
Coloured paper
Felt tip pens
Scissors
Sticky tape
Glue
Optional: plastic animal models
Any other craft materials available

Instructions:
1. First, students need to be able to research where animals might live using books or computers, either as homework or classwork. Animals and habitats could be chosen for each class member, or a list of choices given to them.

Figure 2.1 Habitat diorama – a simple representation of a camel in a desert with a cactus as food

2. Next, set the challenge for students to create a diorama of an animal's habitat. It will need to be accurate and the students can present their models to the class and explain what they have learnt about the habitats.
3. Shoe boxes, cereal boxes or small parcel boxes are excellent bases to build the dioramas on. Plasticine and modelling clay can be used to make the scenery and the living things such as plants.

Health and safety

Hazard and risk	Precautions
Scissors cutting students' hands, hair, clothes, etc.	Adult supervision required. Safety scissors should be used from a reputable supplier.
Sticky tape wrapped around limbs or digits.	Adult supervision required, and any tape wrapped around limbs or digits to be removed immediately.
Plasticine or modelling clay can cause allergies or be swallowed.	Adult supervision required to prevent swallowing of material. All materials should be non-toxic and CE marked for safety. Check allergies before commencing activity.
Paper and cardboard cuts.	Discard any dirty materials. Cereal boxes, etc. need to be in good condition and clean for use in the classroom.

Adapting the activity

Extra support: give students a specific animal to research the habitat of.

Extension: give students the habitat to research, so they can find many living plants or animals in that habitat to include in their diorama and presentation.

Optional extras: explorative questioning such as 'what would happen to the camels if the cacti disappeared from the desert?' to establish that the plants and animals are dependent on each other.

FOOD CHAINS

Equipment:

Pictures that make a food chain, e.g. oak tree with acorn, owl and mouse
Two arrows
String
Scissors
Sticky tape

Instructions:

Lay out the pictures and ask students which order they think the picture go in. Ask questions to stimulate discussion such as 'what does the owl eat?'

Establish that the owl eats the mouse, but the mouse eats the acorn produced by a tree.

Construct a food chain using a vertical piece of string, starting at the bottom of the piece of string with an oak tree and acorn. Add an arrow to show which way the nutrients and energy from the food goes, so it should point at the mouse. Add the mouse to the string, then add another arrow above the mouse pointing to the owl and add the owl in place last.

An alternate version would have an owl with a big circle cut out in the middle, leaving space for a mouse to be suspended inside the owl, with another circle cut out of the mouse leaving room for an acorn. This is simplistic but does show who eats what easily.

Once students get the idea of representing a food chain, they can research their own animals of choice and produce a food chain for them.

Health and safety

Hazard and risk	Precautions
Scissors cutting students' hands, hair, clothes, etc.	Adult supervision required. Safety scissors should be used from a reputable supplier.
Sticky tape wrapped around limbs or digits.	Adult supervision required, and any tape wrapped around limbs or digits to be removed immediately.
String can become wrapped around limbs or pose a suffocation hazard.	Adult supervision required. Only small lengths of string to be distributed to students.
Paper cuts.	Discard any dirty materials. Wash paper cuts if necessary.

Adapting the activity

Extra support: the arrows can be left off the first version while it is established that the plant is eaten by an animal, which is then eaten by another animal.

Extension: ask students where the tree gets its food from to establish where all energy originates from.

Optional extras: construct a human food chain for a vegetarian! Include a parasitic creature on the top of the food chain, e.g. fleas.

Year 2 Plants

National Curriculum Statements:

- observe and describe how seeds and bulbs grow into mature plants;
- find out and describe how plants need water, light and a suitable temperature to grow and stay healthy.

Working scientifically:

- observing closely, using simple equipment;
- performing simple tests;
- using their observations and ideas to suggest answers to questions;
- gathering and recording data to help in answering questions;
- using observations and ideas to suggest answers to questions.

NC Assessment Indicators

Emerging: simply describe how seeds and bulbs grow into mature plants.
Expected: observe and describe observations of plants growing in different conditions.
Exceeding: predict and test what happens to plants lacking in water, light and a suitable temperature.

These activities need to take place over a period of weeks to allow a bulb to grow, but a week will allow cress to grow enough from seed to test how conditions affect the plant.

GROWING PLANTS

Equipment:
Cress seeds

Cotton wool

Clear plastic tubs – reused takeaway tubs are perfect for this/Petri dishes

Any plant which grows from a bulb, e.g. daffodil – preferably purchased as they begin to grow (see garden centres for local availability of bulb based plants)

Thick dark paper or card

Access to a fridge

Water

Instructions:
1. Place the bulb somewhere clear to observe within a classroom. Each day assign a student to observe for any changes and measure any growth of the plant using a ruler.
2. Using plastic tubs or Petri dishes, line the bottom with cotton wool soaked in water. Sprinkle liberally with cress seeds and place in areas with access to sunlight, preferably a windowsill.
3. Observe the cress seeds every day and record their changes verbally, using photography or in short sentences.

GROWING CONDITIONS

Once the cress has grown into short stalks, different growing conditions can be tested to see how they affect the cress.

1. Split the Petri dishes or plastic tubs into four groups.
2. Wrap one group in the thick paper or card to prevent sunlight from reaching the plants. Alternatively, place these plants in a dark cupboard. Be sure to water when the control group is watered to maintain a fair test.
3. Take the second group and place them in the fridge each night, and place them back onto a windowsill for access to sunlight at the start of each school day. This is not an exact test, but it is difficult to maintain sunlight while reducing the temperature in a classroom environment. Water them when the control group is watered.
4. Take the third group and place them on windowsill but do not water this cress! Place a note on the tubs to remind you not to water them.
5. The final group is the control group and should be placed in sunlight and regularly watered – perhaps left where they grew from seed.
6. Compare the groups of cress on a daily basis and record the changes. The results begin to show after a few days and will be quite obvious after a week.

Health and safety

Hazard and risk	Precautions
Cress seeds and cress may be ingested.	Check allergies of pupils before commencing activity, use only under adult supervision. Cress is edible as are the seeds which are eaten in Asia, although care should be taken to prevent children eating the seeds. If cress is stored in a fridge overnight, carefully label as a scientific experiment to prevent consumption by others.
Water spillages can be a slipping hazard.	Clean up any water spillages immediately to prevent slipping hazards.
Glass jars can smash, cling film poses a suffocation hazard.	Adult supervision required as glass can be dropped. Smashed or damaged glass to be discarded immediately. Cling film should be used with adult supervision at all times.

Adapting the activity

Extra support: set up each Petri dish ready for students to place in the appropriate area.

Extension: the height of the cress plants could be recorded before the test and after the test to see the differences in growth during the changes in conditions.

Optional extra: to extend the investigation, access to the air or carbon dioxide could be tested by placing cling film over the tub or a large glass jar over the Petri dish. This will limit the amount of air but take care to water as quickly as possible to limit the effect of fresh air to the cress.

Year 2 Animals including humans

National Curriculum Statements:

- notice that animals, including humans, have offspring which grow into adults;
- find out about and describe the basic needs of animals, including humans, for survival (water, food and air);
- describe the importance for humans of exercise, eating the right amounts of different types of food and hygiene.

Working scientifically:

- using their observations and ideas to suggest answers to questions;
- observing closely, using simple equipment.

NC Assessment Indicators

Emerging: state that animals have offspring.
Expected: describe how offspring change as they become adults, e.g. tadpoles into frogs. Describe the basic needs of animals including humans.
Exceeding: suggest which animals have live young and which lay eggs. Suggest what the animal is from pictures of the offspring. Explain why humans need to exercise, etc.

It is a wonderful idea to hatch a chrysalis into a butterfly for children to observe, or eggs into chicks, however these are season dependant and require great care to protect the living organisms while learning from their growth. If cost is a factor, or animal wellbeing, then a card sort style learning task can still provide active learning. Copyright free images are available from many sources online and can be printed and laminated to be used repeatedly, or printed on cards as a match up activity.

ANIMALS AND THEIR OFFSPRING

Equipment:
Pictures of adult animals, young animals and the egg or new birth animal, e.g. new-born piglet, piglets few months old and adult pigs
Frogspawn, tadpoles, tadpoles with legs growing and frogs
Chicken eggs, chicks and adult chickens

Instructions:
Activity 1
Place pictures around the room for students to collect. Instruct the students to match the animals together, forming a life cycle. Can they recognise the eggs and young? Some students may need hints.

Activity 2
Make the adult and baby or egg pictures as a set of cards. Place the cards face down and take turns to turn over two cards. Do they match? E.g. frog-spawn and frogs. Who can gather the most matching pairs? This activity can be played repeatedly to ensure an understanding of which offspring grow into each adult animal.

Adapting the activity
Extra support: cards can be colour coded into matches to assist students.
Extension: include an intermediate stage between young and adult, e.g. chicken eggs, match chick and adult chickens.
Optional extra: consider similar types of animals, e.g. kittens and tiger cubs. Could discuss similarities between species or vertebrate groups.

KEEPING SOMETHING ALIVE!

If possible, this activity is best done using actual animals such as caterpillars which can be purchased specifically for the purpose of growing a butterfly farm. The caterpillars have to be cared for until they metamorphosise into butterflies. Once grown the butterflies can then be released, so no harm is done to any animals in the experiment.

Alternatively, a thought experiment can be conducted instead.

Equipment:
Pens
Paper
Plasticine or modelling clay

Instructions:
Ask students what they need to survive. If it helps, plan a trip to space or under the sea!

What do they need to take with them to stay alive?

It can be drawn or modelled using modelling clay or plasticine. Hints may be needed such as 'what will you breathe?'

Health and safety

Hazard and risk	Precautions
Plasticine or modelling clay may be consumed by students or cause a slipping hazard if dropped on the floor.	Use under supervision. Avoid contact with mouths and ensure non-toxic. Clear any dropped plasticine or modelling clay immediately.

Adapting the activity

Extra support: the activity could be carried out as a group.

Extension: consider how we keep pets alive – what do we do for them to keep them alive?

Optional extra: consider the gas in the air needed to survive, and the types of food needed, e.g. can I just take chocolate on an adventure into space?

INVESTIGATING THE INTERNATIONAL SPACE STATION

Equipment:

Access to research materials such as computers, books, NASA videos

Instructions:

Investigate the life of an astronaut on the international space station. This could be through independent research, group research, group projects or even video investigation as a class. NASA has produced videos of astronauts on the space station showing how they wash their hair, eat food, exercise and sleep while in space.

Elicit that this is important for all humans, not just astronauts. Consider what would happen if the astronauts in space did not exercise or wash their hair, or if they only ate biscuits and chips. Now relate that to students' own lives. What would happen to them if they did not wash or exercise?

Information can be represented as drawings, cartoons or simple reports.

Adapting the activity

Extra support: the activity could be carried out as a group with directed learning.

Extension: how do astronauts get a balanced diet in space? Find out how astronauts go to the toilet in space!

Optional extra: sample some astronaut food available in shops or online – check allergies first!

Year 2 Uses of everyday materials

National Curriculum Statements:

- identify and compare the suitability of a variety of everyday materials, including wood, metal, plastic, glass, brick, rock, paper and cardboard for particular uses;
- find out how the shapes of solid objects made from some materials can be changed by squashing, bending, twisting and stretching.

Working scientifically:

- performing simple tests;
- identifying and classifying;
- using their observations and ideas to suggest answers to questions.

NC Assessment Indicators

Emerging: identify some suitable materials for a particular use.
Expected: compare the suitability of materials for particular uses with simple tests.
Exceeding: describe how the shapes of solid objects made from some materials can be changed by carrying out practical tests – by squashing, bending, twisting and stretching.

TESTING MATERIALS

Equipment:
Wooden craft sticks
Paper clips
Teaspoons – cheaper metal teaspoons will bend, thicker metal spoons will not bend
Glass beads
Brick pieces
Stones/pebbles
Scrap paper
Cardboard

Metal saucepan/frying pan/cake tin
Elastic bands

Instructions:

Take each material in turn and carry out the following tests. Results can be recorded in a tick table.

Object	Bendy	See-through	Can you squash it?	Can you twist it?	Can you stretch it?

Use the following instructions with the group:

1. Try bending the material with your hands. Does it bend? Hold the object up to the light or a window. Can you see anything through the object? If you can see shadows, objects or people, tick the box. If you cannot see anything through the object, cross the box.
2. Feel the object. Squeeze it gently, then harder. Can you squash it?
3. Hold either end of the object and try to twist it. Can you twist it?
4. Hold either end of the object and pull. Can you stretch it?

Compare the suitability of materials by asking students what would happen if you made a saucepan out of wood? What would happen if you made a saucepan out of stone? Could you still lift it? Students could draw their answers.

Suggested comparisons:

* Would you make a teapot out of paper or metal?
* Would you build a house out of glass, brick or cardboard? What about if it rains? What about if you kick a football inside?
* Which material would you make a window out of? Why?

Health and safety

Hazard and risk	Precautions
Bricks – dust issues with allergies and breathing, sharp edges.	Check allergies of pupils before commencing activity, discard pieces with sharp edges.
Wooden objects can snap and cause splinters.	Discard any snapped wooden objects.
Glass bead can smash.	Adult supervision required as bead can be dropped and broken. Check for chips and damage before using.
Metal spoon and paper clip – metal fatigue and snapping, sharp edges.	Adult supervision required as metal can wear and snap. Check for chips and damage before using. Discard any damaged spoons or paper clips.
Rocks or pebbles can have sharp edges causing cuts, or cause crush injuries though dropping.	Use small pieces of rock or pebbles, discard any with sharp edges, adult supervision required.

Adapting the activity

Extra support: demonstrate how to test each property first or lead the testing in small groups.

Extension: consider the forces that everyday materials must resist, e.g. gravity. What happens if these items are dropped into the floor?

Optional extras: explorative questioning such as 'what is made of wood in the classroom?' 'Why is the window made of glass even though glass can be smashed?'

FURTHER TESTING: COMPARING MATERIALS

Equipment:
Cups
Cup cake cases
Chocolate
Cardboard
Water
Watering can or large bowl
Balsa wood
Coins
Air dry clay
Erasers
Chocolate coins
Aluminium foil
Tin of food
Glass jar or bottle
Ziplock plastic bags × 2

Instructions:

Chocolate cup, teapots, bowls, etc.

Cast a cup shape out of melted chocolate using a large cup and placing a cup cake case in it, before pouring melted chocolate into it. Place another cupcake case on the top and weigh it down gently with another object or substance such as flour, making sure the cupcake cases do not touch. Once set, the chocolate cup shape can be used to demonstrate why chocolate mugs, bowls, teapots, etc. are a bad idea, by pouring hot water on to it.

Cardboard houses

Demonstrate why cardboard is not a good building material by building a model out of it, then placing it in a bowl of water and observing what happens. Alternatively, allow it to 'rain' on the cardboard using a watering can.

Coin carnage

Make a series of 'coins' out of air dry clay, cardboard, balsa wood, erasers and even chocolate coins if they can be acquired. Try making a coin out of aluminium foil. Test the durability of each type of 'currency' by twisting and bending them. Can you pull them apart? Compare to an actual coin!

Glass vs. tins

Compare the advantage of tinned food over glass jars. Choose a food less likely to cause allergic reactions, such as jam or tomato sauce. Place the jar or bottle inside a ziplock bag and close it well. Place inside a second ziplock bag and again close well. With students and staff standing well back, drop the tin of food. It should dent but not split open. Now drop the glass jar or bottle enclosed in bags. The glass should shatter but be contained within the plastic bags.

Health and safety

Hazard and risk	Precautions
Hot water, melted chocolate can cause scalds.	Handled by staff only. Any spillages cleared by staff.
Allergies to chocolate or food products in tins and jars.	Check medical needs before commencing activity. Choose the content of jars and tins sensibly. No food should be consumed in the experiments.
Glass shards can cause cuts and damage faces and eyes.	Staff should use ziplock bags to contain shards of glass. No students or staff should handle the glass shards. Dispose of the broken glass safely.
Water spillages can be a slipping hazard.	Spillages should be cleared immediately.
Balsa wood can splinter, splinters may become embedded in skin.	Use small pieces of wood. Ensure no large splinters before use. Discard once snapped during testing. If a splinter becomes embedded in skin, do not remove it. Consult a first aider.
Erasers, air dry clay, aluminium foil may trigger allergies.	Check medical needs before use. Use under supervision.

Adapting the activity

Extra support: prepare the materials beforehand.

Extension: consider why some are materials are still chosen for a particular use even though they are not the most suitable.

Optional extras: ask students to suggest some materials not suitable for uses that they can then test.

Year 3 Plants

Check for hay fever and plant allergies before completing this activity. Avoid lilies as they often trigger allergies.

MODEL PLANTS

Equipment:
Pipe cleaners in green and white
Thin foam sheets in green and flower colours such as white and red

Orange or yellow plasticine or modelling clay
Scissors
Glue sticks
A complete plant including roots, e.g. a weed from the school grounds –
avoid thorny or spiny plants

Instructions:
Show the class the plant. Explain that each student is going to make a
model of a plant.

1. Give each child a piece of pipe cleaner, approximately 10 cm in length.
   Ask them which part of plant this represents. Ask what the purpose of a
   stem in a plant is. Try to elicit the information that a stem offers support
   and connects the roots to the rest of the plant.
2. Ask students how plants get water from the ground. Ask how they could
   represent the root system of a plant. Give them approximately three
   pieces of white pipe cleaner shorter in length than the green piece.
   These can be attached to the 'stem' by twisting the ends together.
3. Pose the question of what else plants have. Leaves can be represented
   by using green foam cut into leaf shapes. If two ovals are connected by
   a strip of green in between, the leaf shape can be wrapped around the
   stem, doubling up and then secured on the stem by gluing the leaf
   shapes together.

Figure 3.1 Disassembled flower model – these are the components of the flower
model

Figure 3.2 A completed flower model

4. Flowers are created by using coloured foam. Students can cut their own shape of petals, while suggesting why plants need flowers. Squares of foam approximately 6 cm^2 can be provided to students to ensure fair distribution of materials. The flower should be pushed onto the top of the green pipe cleaner, as the metal centre of the pipe cleaner should pierce the foam. This can then be secured by the 'pollen', a piece of modelling clay or plasticine which will also prevent the students stabbing themselves with the sharp end of the pipe cleaner.

Health and safety

Hazard and risk	Precautions
Allergies to plants, flowers, plastic based foam or plasticine and modelling clay. Consumption of plants or plasticine and modelling clay.	Check allergies before commencing the activities. Make sure plants used are not toxic to humans. Plasticine and modelling clay should be non-toxic and used under supervision.
Pipe cleaners can have sharp metal centres causing cuts.	Adult supervision required. When cutting lengths of pipe cleaners, try to ensure clean flat cuts to limit sharp edges. Ensure the top is covered with modelling clay or plasticine to prevent cuts to faces.
Scissors cutting students' hands, hair, clothes, etc.	Adult supervision required. Safety scissors should be used from a reputable supplier.
Glue can be ingested or get in contact with eyes and skin.	Use glue sticks with CE safety mark purchased from reputable suppliers. Adult supervision required.

Adapting the activity

Extra support: give students pictures of a plant with labels for the stem, roots, flowers, petals and pollen.

Extension: students can label their own models or produce a labelled picture to go with their plant.

Optional extras: explorative questioning such as 'do all plants come from seeds?' 'why are flowers pretty' or 'why do they have a smell?' or even 'why don't all plants produce flowers?'

CONDITIONS FOR GROWTH

Equipment:

Plants growing from bulb, already established and in pots × 5 – make sure a grouping of two then three are as similar as possible

Glass bottles or jars with a thinner neck than bottle diameter

Deionised water – available from motoring section of supermarkets

Liquid plant food

Cardboard box

Instructions:

Experiment 1: hydroponics

Hydroponics is the method of growing plants without soil. This investigation allows the exploration of the role of nutrients in plant growth. For this experiment three potted plants growing from bulb are required.

1. Leave one potted plant in its soil in the pot on a windowsill where it has access to light as usual. This is the control plant.
2. Take a second potted plant and gently remove it from the soil.
3. Carefully remove the soil from the roots of the plant being careful not to damage any.
4. Fill the jar or bottle with tepid water and add liquid plant food. Place the bulb of the plant onto the top of a glass jar or bottle. If the top of the jar is too large for the bulb, pad it with cotton wool until it fits on the jar.
5. Place the plant on the windowsill next to the potted plant, ensuring they receive equal amounts of sunlight.
6. Take the third plant and again remove it from the pot gently, ensuring soil is carefully removed from the roots.
7. This time fill a jar or bottle with deionised water – this has no ions or nutrients in it. Place the bulb onto the top of the jar or bottle as before, ensuring the roots are inside the liquid.
8. Again, place the plant on the windowsill with the others, ensuring the same amount of sunlight as the others.
9. Do not forget to water the plant still potted in soil as it has less access to water compared to the other two plants.

10. Observe the growth of the plants after two weeks. Continue observations as long as possible, or until the plant in the deionised water looks less healthy than the other plants. This plant can be revived by adding plant food to the water or placing it back into a pot with soil.

Experiment 2: light and growth
Take two potted plants that are very similar, and place one on a windowsill.

Take a large box and place the second potted plant inside the box. Ensure the plant fits in completely. Close the lid of the box to prevent light entering the box but do allow air movement. Make a hole on the top of the box, to one side, about 5 cm in diameter. Leave the box in an area with access to light through the hole in the box. Do not forget to periodically water the plant, when the first one on the windowsill is watered. Observe after a week. How did the plant respond to the lack of light? What happened to the part of the plant nearest the hole in the box? Compare the plant to the first plant on the windowsill. Repeat the experiment for another week and conduct observations again, comparing to the plant on the windowsill again.

Health and safety

Hazard and risk	Precautions
Allergies to plants, flowers, pollen.	Check allergies before commencing the activities. Make sure plants used are not toxic to humans and the plants are not ingested by students.
Soil can contain microbes and parasites.	Adult supervision required. Hands must be washed after the experiment and before consuming food.
Scissors cutting students' hands, hair, clothes, etc.	Adult supervision required. Safety scissors should be used from a reputable supplier.
Deionised water may be drunk by students.	Although not hazardous, deionised water is not produced for consumption and should not be consumed in any amount. Use under supervision.
Glass jars, vases or beakers can smash and cause cuts.	Adult supervision required. Damaged glass should be discarded immediately.
Water spillages can be a slipping hazard.	Clean water spillages immediately.
Liquid plant food is toxic if ingested.	Use under supervision. Do not allow students to consume the plant food – wash hands after use.

Adapting the activity

Extra support: show pictures of hydroponic growth of plants to introduce the concept.

Extension: students can predict the changes they expect to see in the plants.

Optional extras: explorative hydroponics as a method of producing more food in a smaller space, or even growing plants in space.

TRANSPORT OF WATER IN PLANTS

Equipment:

Celery

Cut flowers, e.g. carnations or similar with white flowers

Dark food colouring such as red or blue – avoid black as it tends to go grey and can be hard to see

Beakers, glass jars or vases

Instructions:

Set up beakers, jars or vases with water in. Add a generous amount of food colouring to the water. Freshly trim the celery and flowers and place them in the water. Leave for a day.

Remove the celery from the water and dry it off. Examine the bottom of the celery. Students can snap the lengths of celery in their hands to see the xylem tubes which carry the water and food colouring up the stem. The xylem are large in celery and easy to distinguish when they have absorbed food colouring.

The longer the flowers are left, the further up the flower stem the food colouring can be transported. If the plant cooperates, the petals may even take on the colour of the water. The flowers can be cut or snapped open to reveal the food colouring in the middle of the plant, showing the path the water is transported along.

Health and safety

Hazard and risk	Precautions
Allergies to plants, flowers. Consumption of plants may cause harm.	Check allergies before commencing the activities. Make sure plants used are not toxic to humans.
Glass jars, vases or beakers can smash and cause cuts.	Adult supervision required. Damaged glass should be discarded immediately.
Water spillages can be a slipping hazard.	Clean water spillages immediately.
Food colouring can cause allergic reactions.	Check for allergies. Do not allow students to consume the water or food colouring.

Adapting the activity

Extra support: set up one experiment to show students and ask what they think has happened. Students can then test their theories by setting up experiments with different colour food colourings.

Extension: the rate of transport of water in the plants can be compared or even timed, with students checking the progress of the food colouring every hour.

Optional extras: does this happen in leaves too? Try it with a flowers stem that has leaves on it. Use a darker food colouring such as purple to investigate this as natural black food colouring tends to go grey and can be hard to see.

THE FLOWER LIFE CYCLE

Equipment:
A fast growing flowering plant such as radish, tomato or cucumber
Compost or a grow bag
Pots or a grow bag tray
A suitable warm, light inside space will mean these can be grown at any time of year

Instructions:
This builds on the knowledge of plants from Years 1 and 2. Students may have grown plants before, but not for the purpose of investigating the role of flowers.

1. Plant the seeds in the compost in pots or in a grow bag depending on the availability at the time of year.
2. Water the seeds periodically until they begin to grow, and consider feeding liquid plant food to them to encourage flower production.
3. Observe the flowers as they develop and open. If it is spring or summer, the flowers will need access to pollinating insects. If this is not possible, then the flowers can be pollinated by hand using a soft paint brush.
4. Once pollinated, a fruit should begin to grow if it is a tomato or a cucumber plant. Radishes grow beneath the soil so may not be obvious. Carefully observe where the fruit is beginning to grow from and watch the changes in the plants daily.
5. Once the fruit has grown and developed, consider how the seeds would be dispersed in nature, in order for the offspring of the plant to grow, e.g. fruit eaten by birds and animals, seeds excreted in their faeces.

Once the life cycle of a plant has been observed, specifically the role of the flower, conclusions can be presented as a report or a poster.

Health and safety

Hazard and risk	Precautions
Allergies to plants, flowers, pollen.	Check allergies before commencing the activities. Make sure plants used are not toxic to humans and the plants are not ingested by students.
Soil can contain microbes and parasites.	Adult supervision required. Hands must be washed after the experiment and before consuming food.
Water spillages can be a slipping hazard.	Clean water spillages immediately.
Liquid plant food is toxic if ingested.	Use under supervision. Do not allow students to consume the plant food – wash hands after use.
Fruit can cause illness if consumed unwashed.	Fruit produced by the plant should not consumed unless washed thoroughly and allergies checked first.

Adapting the activity

Extra support: should the time of year allow, purchase a fruiting plant such as a strawberry and start by observing the fruit, then collecting them and planting the seeds before continuing as before.

Extension: compare seed dispersal in fruiting plants to that of wind dispersed plants such as dandelions. Show pictures of 'dandelion clocks' to stimulate discussion on how those seeds can travel large distances.

Optional extras: visit a 'pick your fruit' farm and investigate how so many fruits are produced. Can the students see traces of the flowers still on the fruit?

Year 3 Animals including humans

National Curriculum Statements:

- identify that humans and some other animals have skeletons and muscles for support, protection and movement;
- identify that animals, including humans, need the right types and amount of nutrition, and that they cannot make their own food; they get nutrition from what they eat.

Working scientifically:

- setting up simple practical enquiries, comparative and fair tests;
- making systematic and careful observations;
- recording findings using simple scientific language, drawings, labelled diagrams, keys, bar charts and tables.

NC Assessment Indicators

Emerging: identify bones and muscles.

Expected: suggest reasons for having a skeleton and muscles.

Exceeding: recognise that bones such as the skull or rib cage protect organs within the body.

ANIMALS AND THEIR FOOD

Equipment:
Cards – one set with a variety of animals on and one set with their foods on OR a set of plastic animals and their food source on cards
Imagination!

Instructions:
Match the animal to its food source, e.g. cattle eat grass and hay, sharks eat fish, whales eat plankton, lions eat meat. Students could go through the options first then play snap where it is only a snap if the animal matches the

food put out. Or, students could play pairs, turning over two cards at a time. If the cards match i.e. it is the animal with its food source, the student keeps the pair, if it does not match, then the student turns the cards back over where they are and it is the next persons go.

Plants vs. animals – a thought experiment!
Imagine you have left on a desert island with a potted plant for company, but there is nothing else there. How long could you survive? How long could the plant survive? Why is there a difference? Plants can make their own food using sunlight but animals have to eat to get their nutrients.

Adapting the activity
Extra support: cards can be colour coded into matches to assist students.
Extension: begin to explore food chains by linking plankton to fish, then fish to sharks.
Optional extra: encourage literacy by including the spellings of the words on the cards.

INVESTIGATING SKELETONS AND MUSCLES

This activity uses food grade animal parts, which could cause discomfort for students that are vegetarian or vegan, or those with eating disorders or sensitivities over food. Students should be offered the chance to observe instead of handling the legs themselves. The parts need to be cooked thoroughly to prevent any infection issues.

Equipment:
Chicken or turkey legs – enough for groups within the class to share
Oven for cooking the meat – including oven trays or roasting dishes
Chopping boards – one per chicken or turkey leg
Scissors

Instructions:
Thoroughly cook the whole chicken or turkey legs keeping the skin soft if possible. Once cooled, students can dissect the chicken or turkey legs using just their fingers, or an adult can cut the skin to start the dissection if necessary.

1. First, holding the two ends of the leg, push on the leg to show how the bones inside the leg can move due to the muscles. Try bending the leg to discover the strength in the bones.
2. Remove the skin to see what is underneath in animals. Identify the meat as muscle within the leg. Pull on the muscles gently to see what happens.
3. Carefully remove the meat/muscles from the bones underneath. Students can feel how hard the bones are.

An adult could carefully snap one of the smaller bones to reveal the bone marrow within the bones.

Health and safety

Hazard and risk	Precautions
Allergies to meat, raw or poorly cooked chicken or turkey poses infection risks.	Check allergies before commencing the activities. Raw chicken or turkey should be kept away from students and handed with care. Hands and contaminated surfaces should be washed afterwards with detergent and hot water. No parts should be consumed at any time, and all parts should be safely disposed of after the activity.
Scissors can cause cuts.	Only adults should use scissors on the legs as they can be slippery with fat.
Chopping boards may be contaminated.	Wash chopping boards thoroughly before and after use with detergent and hot water. Hands should be washed after preparing and completing the activity.
Bones – snapped bones can be sharp. Choking hazard.	Adults can snap bones at their own risk – this should be done away from the face and others. Sharp edges can be examined under adult supervision only. If fully cooked there is no infection risk.

Adapting the activity

Extra support: dissection can be carried out by an adult in small groups so students can observe instead of taking part, or take part when they wish to.

Extension: students can identify the tendons connecting the muscles to the bones, or the cartilage on the end of the bones.

Optional extras: place a cooked bone into a jar of vinegar. The calcium compounds will dissolve as they react with the vinegar, leaving behind the collagen which is bendy. This can help students to understand why calcium in milk and cheese is important in their diet!

Year 3 Rocks

SORTING ROCKS

Equipment:
Class set of rock samples
Plastic beakers
Hand lenses/magnifying glasses
Water

Instructions:

Give each student, or small group of students, an assortment of rocks. First, ask them to sort the rocks into groups based on their appearance. This will be tricky as they have had no other information and many rocks look similar.

Now, students can investigate the appearance and simple physical properties of the rocks by completing a few practical experiments.

Examine the rocks using the hand lenses. Are there crystals? Or are there small holes (called pores) visible?

Hold the rock and squeeze it. Is it hard? Try and scratch the surface with the fingernail. If it will not scratch then it is hard!

Look at the rocks, using hand lenses if necessary. Are there layers visible in the rocks? These might be different coloured stripes, or subtle layers of the same colour.

Place the rocks in a beaker of water. Observe. Are there bubbles coming out of the rock? Some bubbles may appear on the surface when the rock is dropped into the water so try and place them in gently.

Students can complete a tick chart like the one shown below.

Name of rock	Crystals?	Small holes called pores?	Hard?	Layers?	Bubbles in water?

In general, sedimentary rocks have layers and are porous, so bubbles are seen when placed in water. Metamorphic rocks may have layers that are distorted and may have small crystals. Igneous rocks usually do not have layers, and do have crystals, but no pores.

Health and safety

Hazard and risk	Precautions
Rocks may contain microbes and soil contamination. Rocks can also be thrown and cause damage to students, staff and equipment.	Use only under supervision. Hands must be washed after completing the experiments.
Beakers can shatter and cause cuts.	Use under supervision. Plastic beakers are less likely to shatter. Discard any damaged beakers.

Hazard and risk	Precautions
Water spillages can be a slipping hazard, and are a contamination risk if ingested.	Clear any spilt water immediately. Use under supervision, do not allow students to taste or drink the used water.
Hand lenses and magnifying glasses can smash and cause cuts, can magnify sunlight directly into the eye causing blindness or damaged vision.	Use only under supervision. Never look directly at the Sun, especially with hand lenses or magnifying glasses. Do not use in direct sunlight. Discard any damaged or broken hand lenses or magnifying glasses. Check for damage before using.

Adapting the activity

Extra support: demonstrate each part of the experiments to the group. Students can complete one experiment at a time, all together.

Extension: students can compare the weight of rocks using weighing scales before placed in water and after. Sedimentary rocks usually increase in weight as water is absorbed into the pores. These rocks will need time to dry.

Optional extras: shake rock samples in tubs with lids on and see if parts break off easily.

INVESTIGATING SOIL

Equipment:

Soil samples – either from class sets similar to rock sets OR collected from outside

Hand lenses or magnifying glasses

Petri dishes or small plastic containers

Picture of magnified soil samples from reliable source showing shiny rock pieces

Instructions:

Give students small samples of soil and a hand lens or magnifying glass. Ask them to make observations.

Depending on the soil sample and the magnification achieved by the hand lenses or magnifying glasses, students might need to refer to a professionally magnified photograph of soil to see the small rock pieces and the fragments of leaves.

Health and safety

Hazard and risk	Precautions
Soil can contain microbes and parasites.	Use under supervision. Wash hands after use and clean all areas down thoroughly. Do not ingest the soil.
Hand lenses and magnifying glasses can smash and cause cuts, can magnify sunlight directly into the eye causing blindness or damaged vision.	Use only under supervision. Never look directly at the Sun, especially with hand lenses or magnifying glasses. Do not use in direct sunlight. Discard any damaged or broken hand lenses or magnifying glasses. Check for damage before using.

Adapting the activity

Extra support: use a microscope that attaches to a projector/whiteboard if available.

Extension: compare sand to soil – what can students see in the sand when magnified?

Optional extras: make a soil sample using crunchy autumn leaves and small pieces of sandstone or chalk in a jar with a lid. Shake the ingredients up and watch as the leaf disintegrates, and the sandstone and chalk break into tiny fragments.

MODELLING A FOSSIL

Equipment:
Plastic animal models or shells
Plasticine or modelling clay in a variety of colours
Grease proof paper

Instructions:
1. Place a piece of greaseproof paper onto the table to protect the table surface and prevent sticking.
2. Take a small piece of plasticine, about the size of a 50p piece and flatten it onto the greaseproof paper. This is the bottom layer of sediment.
3. Take another colour of plasticine and add small balls of it onto the flat layer. This models more sediment, mud and dust.
4. Add another few layers of small pieces of plasticine of varying colours to the model to build up the layers of sediment.
5. Now, model the animal coming along the mud and dying by placing the plastic animal or shell on to the plasticine layers.
6. More sediment would collect over the body of the animal, so place more plasticine pieces onto the plastic animal or shell.
7. Over time, these layers get compressed so, press down on the stack of plasticine and squash the layers all together.

8. Now peel apart the plasticine carefully to reveal the plastic animal or shell. Remove the plastic animal or shell by only touching the edges. An imprint should remain behind. This is model of a fossil!

Health and safety

Hazard and risk	Precautions
Allergies to plasticine or modelling clay, staining from the colourings used.	Check allergies before commencing activities. Wash hands after use, use only CE marked non-toxic products.
Plastic animals or shells swallowed or snapped causing cuts.	Adult supervision required. Discard any damaged items.

Adapting the activity

Extra support: prepare the plasticine pieces before the activity for those with motor difficulties.

Extension: students can try and match the imprints in the plasticine to the animals that formed them by examining the detail in the imprints.

Optional extras: the imprints or 'fossils' can be cast using plaster of Paris, but only by an adult as plaster of Paris is an exothermic reaction and can be harmful. A risk assessment must be carried out.

Year 3 Light

National Curriculum Statements:

- recognise that they need light in order to see things and that dark is the absence of light;
- notice that light is reflected from surfaces;
- recognise that light from the Sun can be dangerous and that there are ways to protect their eyes;
- recognise that shadows are formed when the light from a light source is blocked by an opaque object;
- find patterns in the way that the size of shadows changes.

Working scientifically:

- setting up simple practical enquiries, comparative and fair tests;
- making systematic and careful observations;
- identifying differences, similarities or changes related to simple scientific ideas and processes.

NC Assessment Indicators

Emerging: recognise that shadows form when light from a light source is blocked by an opaque object. Recognise that light is needed to see things.

Expected: recognise that the distance between the light source and the object affects the size of the shadows. Recognise that light from the Sun can be dangerous.

Exceeding: predict whether a shadow will be larger or smaller when the position of the light source changes.

MIRROR MAGIC

Equipment:
Small mirrors with a flat edge
Blu tack or plasticine
2D shapes

Instructions:
Place the mirror on its flat edge and secure it with blu tack or plasticine to hold it 90 degrees from the paper. Make sure the mirror is perpendicular to the student.

Place the mirror in this position half way across a 2D shape to explore the reflection. What happens if you place it on an asymmetrical shape?

Explore the alphabet – which letters look the same in a mirror?

Can you write a message that can only be read in a mirror?

Health and safety

Hazard and risk	Precautions
Glass mirrors can shatter and cause cuts. Direct sunlight can be reflected into eyes and cause damage to vision.	Use plastic mirrors if available. Discard damaged glass mirrors and clear up smashed glass immediately. Avoid use in direct sunlight.
Plasticine or blu tack can pose a choking hazard.	Use under supervision, avoid contact with the mouth.

Adapting the activity
Extra support: examine reflections as a small group. Provide a printed alphabet for students to examine in a mirror.
Extension: use the mirrors to complete symmetrical drawings by placing against the half already drawn and using the mirror to see the shape of the object.
Optional extras: investigate the number of lines of symmetry in shapes.

VIEWING THE SUN SAFELY WITH PINHOLE CAMERAS

Equipment:
Solar viewing glasses if available
Small cardboard box such as single serving cereal box
Tracing paper
Scissors
Sticky tape
Pencil
A light bulb in the room

Instructions:

Looking directly at the Sun is dangerous and can damage the eyes permanently.

If solar viewing glasses are available, these can be used to view the Sun directly if worn correctly. If you do not have any, there is still a way to view the Sun and eclipses.

1. Cut the flaps off the top of the small cardboard box leaving the top open.
2. Cut a piece of tracing paper the right size to cover the top of the box and fold over the sides for approximately 1 cm.
3. Carefully secure the tracing paper in place using sticky tape around the edges, avoiding sticking over the top of the box.
4. Turn the box over and carefully pierce the card using a sharp pencil. The hole needs to be the diameter of an average pencil.
5. Test the pinhole camera by holding it half an arm's length away from the face and aiming the small hole at a light bulb. Students should only look at the tracing paper and should see the light bulb on the surface of the tracing paper. It might take some adjustment to achieve the right distance to view the picture on the tracing paper.
6. To view any strong light source such as the Sun, students must stand to one side to view the tracing paper rather than directly behind it, to avoid any accidental direct exposure to the Sun.

Health and safety

Hazard and risk	Precautions
Small cardboard boxes causing card/paper cuts, as can tracing paper.	Use clean card and paper for this project.
Light bulb may get hot or damage eyes. The Sun can cause blindness.	Adults and students should not look directly into the light and NEVER directly at the Sun unless wearing solar viewing glasses certified for that use. Do not touch the light bulb.
Scissors cutting students' hands, hair, clothes, etc.	Adult supervision required. Safety scissors should be used from a reputable supplier.
Sticky tape can become entangled on limbs or digits.	Adult supervision required. Any sticky tape on limbs or digits should be removed immediately.

Adapting the activity

Extra support: pre-cut the boxes for students. Provide several light sources such as torches to test the pinhole cameras with.

Extension: use a filament bulb with the pinhole camera to examine the image. Is it the right way up?

Optional extras: can you use the theory to make any other types of pinhole cameras? Do larger pinhole cameras work?

LIGHT: SHADOW PUPPETS

Equipment:
Tissue paper
Thick card or a large cardboard box
Thin card
Wooden craft sticks
Sticky tape
Lamp or torch

Instructions:
Use the thick cardboard to make a large frame, or cut the top flaps off a large box, then cut out the bottom of the box, leaving approximately 5 cm around the edge of the sides of the box. Cover the gap with a flat piece of tissue paper. Stretch it over the gap then secure it with sticky tape. This will be the shadow puppet theatre.

After a discussion with the students about how shadows form, demonstrate how the shadow theatre works using a ready-made puppet.

Students can then design their own shadow puppet and cut it out of the thin card. Remind them that it is only the outside edge, the silhouette, that will be seen. Stick the card shape onto a wooden craft stick, leaving a long handle for the students to hold.

Place the torch or lamp behind the shadow puppet theatre and let students experiment with the puppets between the lamp and the theatre, with the other students watching the shadows from the other side.

Now, ask the students what will happen if the torch is moved closer to the shadow puppets. Move the lamp closer and see what difference it makes. Ask the students what will happen when the lamp is moved further away from the shadow puppets. Move the lamp and observe the difference.

Extra: see what difference the angle of the lamp makes to the shadows. Can you make them appear taller or shorter?

Figure 3.3 Shadow puppets – simple outlines cut out of card and secured to a wooden craft stick using sticky tape

Health and safety

Hazard and risk	Precautions
Thin card and thick card edges causing cuts.	Use clean card for this project.
Lamp or torch may get hot or damage eyes.	Adults and students should not look directly into the light. Do not touch the light bulb.
Scissors cutting students' hands, hair, clothes, etc.	Adult supervision required. Safety scissors should be used from a reputable supplier.
Sticky tape can become entangled on limbs or digits.	Adult supervision required. Any sticky tape on limbs or digits should be removed immediately.

Adapting the activity

Extra support: pre-cut shapes could be provided for the students.

Extension: measure the distance between the lamp and the shadow puppet, then measure the length or width of the shadow cast on the theatre screen. Now move the lamp 10 cm closer and measure the shadow again. This can be repeated, and data represented as a graph.

Optional extras: turn the activity into a cross-curricular opportunity and play out a story on the shadow theatre!

Year 3 Forces and magnets

National Curriculum Statements:

- observe how magnets attract or repel each other and attract some materials and not others;
- compare and group together a variety of everyday materials on the basis of whether they are attracted to a magnet, and identify some magnetic materials.

Working scientifically:

- setting up simple practical enquiries, comparative and fair tests;
- making systematic and careful observations;
- using results to draw simple conclusions, make predictions for new values, suggest improvements and raise further questions;
- using straightforward scientific evidence to answer questions or to support their findings.

NC Assessment Indicators

Emerging: use results to make simple conclusions on which everyday materials are magnetic.

Expected: make predictions for whether other materials are magnetic or not.

Exceeding: predict what everyday materials are magnetic by recognising what they are made of.

ATTRACTING MAGNETIC MATERIALS

Equipment:
Paper clips
Staples
Pencil
Wooden craft stick
Iron nail
Penny
Glass bead
Plastic bead
Plastic animal
Rock or stone
Rubber eraser
Metal teaspoons
Steel wool scouring pads
Jar lids
Any other suitable materials
Magnets

Instructions:
Separate out the materials into class sets of each material. Students could predict which materials might be magnetic.

1. Hold the magnet gently touching the material.
2. Raise the magnet and observe if the item is lifted by the magnet. If it is lifted, the item is magnetic!
3. Place all the magnetic items together in a group.
4. Pose the question 'what are all of these materials made of?'

Health and safety

Hazard and risk	Precautions
Mixed materials – breaking, cutting skin.	Use clean, undamaged objects. Discard any damaged objects.
Magnets – interfering with medical devices, small magnets can be swallowed and cause choking.	Be aware of any medical devices in students or staff before handling magnets. Use under supervision. School magnets are often small squares coated in blue and red plastic ends which can come apart, remove from use if this occurs.

Be aware of the dangers of magnetic putty if not purchased from a reliable supplier, and the potential for choking and allergies to magnetic putty or slime. This is not a material recommended for this experiment.

Adapting the activity

Extra support: sort materials into piles of plastic, wood and metals to begin with, for easier comparison or sorts of materials.

Extension: include aluminium foil and a variety of drinks cans or small sealed tins of food to include more types of metal. Steel drinks cans are usually labelled as steel on the packaging and will be magnetic. Aluminium cans are much lighter and not magnetic.

Optional extras: labelled metal strips may be in the science cupboard and could be used to determine that not all metals are magnetic, but specifically iron and steel are.

Year 4 Living things and their habitats

National Curriculum Statements:

- recognise that living things can be grouped in a variety of ways;
- explore and use classification keys to help group, identify and name a variety of living things in their local and wider environment;
- recognise that environments can change and that this can sometimes pose dangers to living things.

Working scientifically:

- using straightforward scientific evidence to answer questions or to support their findings;
- making systematic and careful observations;
- recording findings using simple scientific language, drawings, labelled diagrams, keys, bar charts and tables.

NC Assessment Indicators

Emerging: group living things in a variety of ways, with prompts.
Expected: use a classification key to identify common living things around the school. Recognise dangers to living things posed by changing environments.
Exceeding: construct a simple classification key, suggest dangers to living things posed by changing environments.

GROUPING LIVING THINGS

Equipment:

Picture cards of various plants and animals, e.g.:

  Oak tree

  Apple tree

  Birch tree

  Fir tree

  Blackberry bush

  Hawthorn bush

  Sunflower

  Poppy

  Rose bush

  Grasshopper

  Moth

  Sheep

  Cow

  Chicken

  Fish

  Green frog

  Stick insect

  Dandelion

Instructions:

Sets of cards can be distributed to small groups of students, alternatively, assign one card per student and they can physically sort themselves by moving around the room.

Ask students to sort the living things into groups. A prompt may be required for the first sort – plants and animals is a good demonstration of one possible grouping.

Students can then suggest ways of grouping themselves. Here is a brief list of suggestions and examples:

Sort by colour – green animals and plants together.

Sort by size – trees, bushes, animals, insects.

Sort by kingdom and then vertebrates, invertebrates and finally vertebrate group, using knowledge from Year 2.

Sort by number of legs – plants have no legs, sheep and cows have four, insects have six.

DESIGN YOUR OWN CLASSIFICATION KEY

Your school may already have classification keys for the school field or trees, so these can be used as an introduction to the concept, with this activity to extend the learning and understanding.

Equipment:

Pictures of common animals found around the school, e.g.:

Snail

Blackbird

Hedgehog

Squirrel

Butterfly

Common cartoon characters or book characters from a book the class has been reading

Instructions:

Demonstrate how to begin a branching classification key with closed questions that can either be answered with a yes or no, e.g. 'does it have wings?' 'yes' leads to the next question. 'Does it have a beak?''yes' leads to the answer blackbird, 'no' leads to the answer butterfly.

Students can then use the pictures to construct their own classification key, either as an individual piece of classwork gluing pictures to paper, or as a giant display piece using small whiteboards to pose the questions on.

To deepen the understanding, the students can then be challenged to design a harder classification key, using similar characters from a cartoon or book, where the characters are all versions of an animal or human, for example. Questions would need to be more specific to recognise the subtle differences between living things in this case. More able students may construct a statement key instead.

Adapting the activity

Extra support: introduce students to trees or plants in the school grounds, naming each one and collecting a sample of a leaf so students can associate the shapes with the tree or plant names.

Extension: students can collect leaves from around the school grounds, then construct a key type of their choice, and make a key using those leaves.

Optional extras: students may construct branching or statement keys using objects in the classroom, then see if their peers can correctly identify the objects to practice using a key.

ENVIRONMENTAL CHANGE

Equipment:

Colouring pens or pencils

Paper – page split into two halves by a dividing line with the same animal on both sides of the page

Instructions:

On the left side of the paper ask the student to draw the normal habitat for that animal, e.g. a polar bear might be on ice. On the right side, ask them to imagine there was no more ice – what would happen to the habitat?

A squirrel might be in a tree, but what happens if there are no more trees?

Any animal can be chosen for this activity.

Adapting the activity

Extra support: start with the left side of the paper already showing the correct habitat for the animal.

Extension: students can suggest what could change in the environment to affect the habitat, e.g. if it gets warmer and ice melts, or if the food disappears.

Optional extras: explore natural environmental change such as the change in seasons too.

Year 4 Animals including humans

Check for hay fever and plant allergies before completing this activity, or insect stings and bite allergies.

MODELLING THE DIGESTIVE SYSTEM

Equipment:
Ziplock plastic bags
Clean tights – thick and thin
Pestle and mortar
Large clear tubing if possible

Spoons

A plastic table cloth or tray to conduct the experiment over

'Saliva' and 'stomach acid' – labelled jugs but containing just water for health and safety reasons (lemon juice could be added to the 'acid' so it really smells acidic)

Washing up bowl

Food samples – banana, cooked green leafy vegetables and chocolate wheat biscuit cereal or chocolate milk are a good mix to achieve realistic colour and smell

Video clip of an animal chewing food

Instructions:

This can either be done as a clean model on the wall as a display, or as a model that gets used (take photographs for a later display) or make two models allowing the students to join in the practical, and do both! The pictures can help stimulate the creative descriptive writing that goes with this project!

Discuss the first thing that happens to the food you eat. Use mirrors to look inside your own mouth – what is in your mouth? Teeth, spit, etc. What happens when you chew? Watch a video clip of a cow or giraffe chewing to see that the mouth turns food round while chewing. Model this action with a pestle and mortar to chew the food samples. Do not forget to add 'saliva' to make it easier to swallow!

Use a large clear tube if you have one and pour the chewed food down the tube into the clear ziplock bag. This represents the oesophagus and stomach! If you do not have a tube, just pour it from a height to represent the distance it travels. Discuss what happens in the stomach, and then add some 'stomach acid' to the bag before zipping it closed and churning it up using your hands. Pupils can help at this point, churning the food in the bag.

Where does food go from here? What changes between the way it looks now and the way it looks when we excrete the waste? Discuss the change in colour, shape, state of matter, etc.

Now model the small intestine using some tights with the tops and the foot cut off to form a tube – this is where more enzymes are added and nutrients in our food are absorbed into the blood. Gently spoon the food from the ziplock bag into the tights and slowly push it through the tights. Try not to lose too much liquid at this point.

The large intestine can be modelled in the same way with thinner tights, but leave the foot attached. Ask pupils what needs to happen here to make the waste (nutrients have been absorbed) look like poo. Squeeze the tights to make the water/liquid come out of the waste – use a washing up bowl to catch any mess.

Discuss what happens to waste our bodies do not need, then cut the foot part of the tights open and squeeze out the semi-solid waste!

Pupils can describe the process in sentences using writing frames, key words or their own writing skills. These descriptions can be stuck in a display, or written around a photograph showing what pupils did.

Health and safety

Hazard and risk	Precautions
Allergies to food samples.	Check allergies before commencing the activities.
Pestle and mortar.	Use under supervision, check for damage before use
Stomach acid and saliva – risk of infections, slipping on spillages, acid burns.	Use only water with labels that state 'saliva' or 'stomach acid'. Clear up any spillages immediately.
Plastic bags – risk of suffocation.	Use only under supervision and safely discard of after the activity. If plastic is avoided in this environment, use a large mixing bowl instead and do not use a plastic tube.
Tights – suffocation and strangulation risk.	Use only under adult supervision. Cut the tights so it is just the leg section for use – this limits the length available and reduces risk.
Scissors cutting students' hands, hair, clothes, etc.	Adult supervision required. Safety scissors should be used from a reputable supplier.

Adapting the activity

Extra support: this could be a complete modelling activity where pupils spectate or complete small parts of the practical.

Extension: include indigestible foods such as sweetcorn which can then be identified in the waste matter at the end.

Optional extras: students can perform the mechanical digestion using pestle and mortars and the stomach churning in 'acid', combining their products in one big bowl for the teacher to demonstrate the intestines. Alternatively, allow students to carry out the whole experiment.

MODELLING TEETH

Equipment:
Air dry clay – enough for a whole class to make four models approximately 5 cm in height
Plasticine or fruit such as apples and bananas – depending on allergies

Instructions:
There are three types of teeth, each with a different job.

The very front teeth are incisors and are for biting. Students can make a model of an incisor tooth using air dry clay, formed into a spade shape. The model needs to be big enough to use the tooth after it has dried.

Canines are for biting. These look like incisors but have a pointed end for tearing and ripping food.

Molars are for grinding and are much wider and flatter, for grinding food. Students will need to construct two of these.

Once the models have dried and become hard, students can use them for their intended job by pressing the incisors into the food or plasticine and seeing if it goes through. Pull a canine tooth model through the food or plasticine and see if it tears through the medium. Now try the molar models. Place some food or plasticine between two molars and grind the two together. What happens to the food?

Students can represent their findings on posters with diagrams or photographs.

Health and safety

Hazard and risk	Precautions
Allergies to food samples.	Check allergies before commencing the activities. Only use foods that students have no allergies to, or use plasticine instead.
Air dry clay – allergies, clay stuck to hair, clothes, risk of eating.	Use under supervision. Clay should be non-toxic and usually take several days to dry, so can be cleaned off items and students before it hardens. Allergies should be checked before using.
Model teeth can snap or shatter causing cuts.	Use under supervision. Models should be made large enough to handle afterwards.

Adapting the activity

Extra support: students could build the part of the tooth they can see and ignore the root for this activity.

Extension: include the long roots of adult teeth in the experiment to show how teeth can be so strong.

Optional extras: students can construct models of other teeth such as shark teeth to see how they are adapted to their function.

Year 4 States of matter

SOLIDS, LIQUIDS AND GASES

Equipment:
Samples in a closed container or tub, etc.:
   Water, cooking oil, vinegar, syrup, honey
   Tubs of sand and salt
   Sealed plastic tubes labelled 'air', 'oxygen', 'carbon dioxide'
   Wooden blocks
   Marbles
   Plasticine or play dough
   Plastic bricks
   Chalk
   Other materials available in the classroom
Demonstration only – tealight candle, beaker, sodium bicarbonate, vinegar
Round balloon
Long balloon
Water balloons

Instructions:
This experiment can be conducted in small groups or as a larger group.

Ask students to group the materials into solids, liquids and gases. Ask for justification for each material, e.g. 'how do you know it is a solid?'

Examine which materials can be poured by tipping up the sealed containers. Pose the question 'Is it only liquids that can be poured?'. Small pieces of solids can also be poured – salt, sand.

Light the tealight out of reach of the students. Place two tablespoons of sodium bicarbonate into a beaker. Add a large splash of vinegar and tip the beaker into a pouring position over the candle, without pouring out the solution. The carbon dioxide will pour out of the beaker and flow over the candle, extinguishing the flame. This is because carbon dioxide is denser than air.

Can the material take the shape of its container? Place each material in a bowl. Does it change shape? The solids sand and salt will take the shape of the bowl BUT the individual pieces of sand or salt do not change shape. Inflate the round balloon – the air takes a round shape. Now inflate the long balloon – it is a different shape to the round balloon. Why? Gases take the shape of their container.

Can you change the amount of space or volume a material takes? Try squashing the plastic brick, marble and wooden block. Now try squashing the plasticine. It will squash, but if you put it back into the original shape, it still takes up the same volume. Try filling some water balloons half full. Measure the amount of water you fill them with. Try squashing the water balloons. Now carefully open the water balloons and measure how much water there is. The volume should be the same!

Try squashing the air balloons. The air can be compressed and squashed, the volume can be changed.

Challenge students to represent all the properties of the state of matter as a poster!

Health and safety

Hazard and risk	Precautions
Mixed materials including plasticine or play dough can cause allergies or be consumed.	Check allergies before commencing the activities. Use under supervision, no materials should be consumed during the experiment.
Tealight candle, flames can burn.	This is a demonstration activity only – this should not be done by students due to the risk of burns. Ensure another means to extinguish flame such as a fire blanket or fire bucket is near. Carry out the experiment on a surface that is not flammable and is away from the reach of students.
Balloons and water balloons are a choking hazard.	Use under supervision. Plastic pieces should be carefully discarded after use. Balloons are single use to prevent contamination.

Adapting the activity

Extra support: begin with an inflated balloon, a beaker of water and a wooden block to establish the difference between solids, liquids and gases.

Extension: include materials such as jelly, which is a colloid and neither a liquid or a solid but with properties of both.

Optional extras: try different shaped containers to establish if the materials take the shape of their containers – ice cube trays can be purchased in different shapes.

CHANGING STATE WITH CHOCOLATE

Equipment:
White chocolate buttons
Milk chocolate buttons
Dark chocolate buttons or drops
Thermometers

Warm water
Large bowls
Beakers or plastic tubes

Instructions:

Practice may be required with reading a thermometer before this activity, and basic knowledge of the change of states. Begin by questioning the students on how can conduct a fair test, to elicit the importance of using the same amount of chocolate each time.

Students may even make a prediction for which chocolate will melt at a lower temperature!

1. Place five white chocolate buttons into a plastic tube or beaker. Place a thermometer into the tube, touching the chocolate.
2. Lower the tube into a large bowl of warm water ensuring no water enters the tube.
3. Observe the chocolate and record the temperature on the thermometer when the chocolate has melted.
4. Repeat the experiment with milk chocolate in a clean tube if the same size, and again with dark chocolate, ensuring the same amount of chocolate is used. Fresh warm water may be needed for each experiment.

Students can construct a graph to compare the melting points of the chocolate.

Health and safety

Hazard and risk	Precautions
Chocolate – allergies if consumed, contamination of chocolate.	Check allergies before commencing the activities. Use under supervision, no materials should be consumed during the experiment.
Warm water can cause scalds, slipping on spilt water.	It is vital that the water is not hot enough to cause scalds. Most chocolate melts at around body temperature, so 40°C should be warm enough for the experiment and limit danger to students and staff. Spillages should be cleaned up immediately.
Thermometers can break, and the glass can pierce the skin.	Use under supervision. Ensure modern thermometers containing alcohol are used. Discard any damaged thermometers.
Plastic tubes or beakers, large bowls – can still shatter and pierce skin.	Plastic is less likely to shatter than glass so is the safer option. Discard any damaged items and use under supervision.

Adapting the activity

Extra support: compare the melting point of an ice cube with the melting point of chocolate to demonstrate that different materials have different melting points, and to show a change of state.

Extension: the reverse of the experiment could be performed, cooling the chocolate in a bowl of ice water and measuring the temperature as the chocolate solidifies.

Optional extras: compare different brands of chocolate, or chocolate composites such as common chocolate treats.

PUDDLE PRACTICALS

Equipment:
Shallow tubs or Petri dishes
Jug or measuring cylinder
Water

Instructions:
Basic knowledge of the water cycle is needed prior to this activity, which takes place over several days depending on conditions.

Pose the question 'What happens to a puddle after it rains?' students should acknowledge that puddles disappear due to evaporation.

Ask students to predict whether puddles disappear quicker when it is warmer or colder. Students can then test their prediction with experimental observations.

1. Collect three shallow tubs of the same size. Place a small amount of water in each tub – ensure the amount of water is the same in each tub for a fair test, using a jug or measuring cylinder. These are the puddles.
2. Select three places the tubs could be placed that have different temperatures, e.g. the fridge, on the windowsill and next to a heater.
3. Leave the tubs of water and observe the levels of water at the beginning of each day, half way through the day and at the end of each day to determine which temperature allowed the puddle to evaporate first.

Students can present their findings in a written format, including whether their prediction was correct.

Health and safety

Hazard and risk	Precautions
Water spillages can be a slipping hazard.	Clean up any water spillages immediately to prevent slipping hazards.
Jugs, measuring cylinders, shallow tubs and Petri dishes can shatter and cause cuts.	All equipment should be plastic and discarded if damaged.

Adapting the activity

Extra support: begin by demonstrating puddle evaporation, by pouring a jug of water outside the classroom and seeing if it is still there at the end of the day, or by the next day.

Extension: the temperature could be measured in each area chosen for the tubs, and a timer could be set to record the number of hours each puddle takes to evaporate. The activity could also be extended by comparing the different sized 'puddles' in each area.

Optional extras: construct a plasticine scene for the puddle to make it more realistic, placing the tub or Petri dish into the plasticine model.

Year 4 Sound

National Curriculum Statements:

- identify how sounds are made, associating some of them with something vibrating;
- recognise that vibrations from sounds travel through a medium to the ear;
- find patterns between the pitch of a sound and features of the object that produced it;
- find patterns between the volume of a sound and the strength of the vibrations that produced it.

Working scientifically:

- setting up simple practical enquiries, comparative and fair tests;
- recording findings using simple scientific language, drawings, labelled diagrams, keys, bar charts and tables;
- identifying differences, similarities or changes related to simple scientific ideas and processes;
- using straightforward scientific evidence to answer questions or to support their findings.

NC Assessment Indicators

Emerging: identify vibrations as being associated with sound and that they travel to the ear.

Expected: find patterns between features of objects that produce sound and the pitch or volume of the sound.

Exceeding: predict how the sound will change when changes are made to the instrument producing the sound.

LISTENING TO SOUNDS

Equipment:
A plastic bottle filled with water
A plastic bottle filled with sand
A plastic bottle filled with air
Tables

Instructions:
We can hear sound through the air, but can we hear sound through a solid? In pairs, one student places their ear against the table, and the other student gently taps the table with their fingertip. Can the first student hear it? Now, one student holds the bottle of sand next to their ear. The other student gently taps the other side of the bottle. Did they hear the noise?

Repeat this using the bottle of water. Can they hear the sound travel?

Now try with the bottle of air. Can they hear the sound now?

Which bottle let the sound travel the easiest or loudest, or was the table a better transmitter of sound?

The particles in the table are so close together that they transmit sound easily and with little energy loss.

Health and safety

Hazard and risk	Precautions
Sensitivity to sound – activity could cause distress.	Check the medical needs of students before commencing the activity. Those with sensitive hearing may wish to observe the activities or complete them on their own so they have control over the noises.
Spillages from the bottles leaking can be a slipping hazard.	Clean up any spillages immediately. Ensure lids are fitted tightly to bottles.

Adapting the activity
Extra support: begin by demonstrating sound travelling to the ears by covering the ears to see if it affects how the sound is heard.
Extension: see how gently the objects must be tapped to still be heard though the material.
Optional extras: compare different thicknesses of liquids. Explore the idea of particle arrangement in relation to the state of matter to help explain why solids transmit sound better than liquids or gases.

STRAW FLUTES

Equipment:
Plastic straws – this will not work with paper straws as the material has to be rigid enough to vibrate
Scissors

Instructions:
This can take a while to master as the technique is very tricky!

1. Flatten the edge of a plastic straw using the finger tips, then cut it into a steep point like a spear.
2. Place the spear end of the straw with the points vertical to each other into the mouth and press down gently with the lips. The position may need to be adjusted to achieve the noise and does take practice! It is most like playing a flute, less like a recorder.
3. Blow into to the straw and slowly move the straw further out of the mouth until the straw omits a shrill noise. Usually, the cut V shape should be just inside the lips, but it is slightly different for everyone.
4. Once the noise has been mastered, students can shorten the length of their straw flute by cutting from the bottom of the straw and observe the difference it makes to the pitch.

Straw flutes work as the air from the lungs vibrates the sharp tips, which in turn push air particles into the straw, bouncing them off the sides of the straw all the way down the straw. These vibrations then enter the air around the straw and travel to our ears.

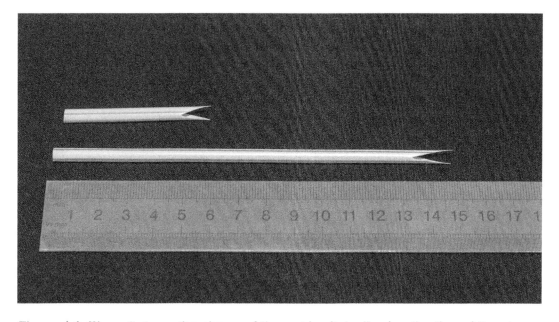

Figure 4.1 Straw flutes – the shape of the cut is vital, allowing the tips of the straw to vibrate

Health and safety

Hazard and risk	Precautions
Plastic straws – contamination risk from multiple use, environmental hazard, sharp point will be cut with scissors and could stab the mouths of students and can pose a choking risk.	Plastic straws are single use and must be disposed of carefully to reduce the risk of environmental pollution. Straw flutes should be used only under supervision and students should sit in seats to reduce the risk of falling over and choking on straws or knocking themselves and stabbing their mouths with sharp points.
Sensitivity to sound – activity could cause distress.	Check the medical needs of students before commencing the activity. Those with sensitive hearing may wish to observe the activities or complete them on their own so they have control over the noises.
Scissors cutting students' hands, hair, clothes, etc.	Adult supervision required. Safety scissors should be used from a reputable supplier.

Adapting the activity

Extra support: students may need the straws cut into shape for them as this requires fine motor skills.

Extension: construct different lengths of straw flutes secured together like pan pipes to easily compare the difference in pitch.

Optional extras: compare the straw flutes to reed instruments to explain how the vibrations of the tips cause the noise.

STRING INSTRUMENT DEMONSTRATION

Equipment:
Plastic cups or plastic beakers
Elastic bands
Pencil

Instructions:
Place an elastic band over the beaker or cup vertically so it crosses the open end. Strum the elastic band so it makes a twang noise.

Now tuck the pencil between the elastic band and the cup. The pencil can now be turned to tighten the elastic band as it twists around the pencil. Strum again and observe the difference pitch. Repeat several times but ensure this has been practised beforehand to establish how far the elastic bands will stretch before snapping.

Can students make a conclusion linking how tightly stretched the elastic band is to the pitch produced?

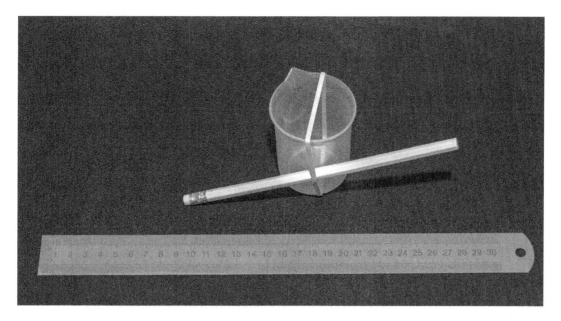

Figure 4.2 String instrument model – it is easier to place the pencil between the side of the plastic beaker and the elastic band. Plastic beakers are stronger than plastic cups so the elastic band can be twisted tighter, and the equipment is reusable after the experiment

Health and safety

Hazard and risk	Precautions
Plastic cups or beakers can shatter and cause cuts.	Adult supervision required, discard damaged items immediately.
Elastic bands can snap and damage eyes or skin.	Practice the activity to establish the approximate strength of the elastic bands in use in the classroom. The practical should be carried out away from the face, on the table or at arm's length.
Pencils can snap and cause splinters.	Adult supervision required. Discard broken pencils.

Adapting the activity

Extra support: students may need the cup, elastic band and pencil set up for them.

Extension: compare different sized elastic bands on different shaped plastic cups or beakers.

Optional extras: examine a guitar or ukulele to see that the strings are tightened to change their pitch.

RECYCLED INSTRUMENTS

Equipment:
Card from the recycling pile, e.g. cereal boxes
Plastic bottles with lids
Yogurt pots
Elastic bands
balloons
String
Beads, rice or dried peas
Sticky tape
Scissors

Instructions:
Students can construct their own instruments using the pile of materials and their imagination. They may need to see pictures of instruments to stimulate ideas.

As a guide, elastic bands and string can be used to construct stringed instruments like guitars, while beads, rice and dried beads can become shakers. Balloons can be pulled over plastic pots and secured with elastic bands to construct drums.

All of these instruments have vibrations in common. Once constructed, ask students to play their instruments hard – either strumming hard or shaking hard or hitting the drum hard to see how it affects the volume being produced by the instruments.

Health and safety

Hazard and risk	Precautions
Recycling materials such as cardboard or plastic may pose contamination risk.	Use clean, washed items only. Discard any damaged or dirty items immediately.
Sticky tape can become wrapped around limbs.	Adult supervision required, remove immediately from limbs.
Scissors cutting students' hands, hair, clothes, etc.	Adult supervision required. Safety scissors should be used from a reputable supplier.
Elastic bands can snap and damage eyes or skin	Adult supervision required.
Dried peas, beads or rice may pose choking risk or slip hazard if spilt, may also cause allergic reaction.	Adult supervision required. Avoid items being placed in the mouth. Clear up spillages immediately. Check allergies before using dried peas or rice.
Balloons may cause allergic reaction and pose a choking hazard, risk of contamination.	Balloons are single use and must not be passed between students. Check allergies before handling. Use under supervision.

Adapting the activity

Extra support: show students some examples of what they could construct.

Extension: ask students 'how many different ways can sound be produced?'

Optional extras: use a decibel meter or smart phone app to measure the volume of sound produced.

Year 4 Electricity

CIRCUITS: CONDUCTORS AND INSULATORS

Equipment:
Wire with crocodile clips × 3
Bulb
Battery in battery holder
Metal spoon
Metal paper clip
Metal nail
Plastic spoon
Wooden craft stick
Plastic brick
Wooden block

Glass marble or bead

Aluminium foil

Pencil

Other suitable classroom objects

Instructions:

This can be done in small groups or as a large demonstration. Pupils can predict the outcome before the materials are tested, potentially completing a table, which can later be compared to actual results.

Connect both side of the battery to a wire. Connect one of the wires from the battery to the bulb, connect the third wire to the other side of the bulb. Ensuring crocodile clip connectors are on the unconnected wires, materials can be clipped between them and the bulb observed. If the bulb lights up, the object is a conductor. If it does not light up and the circuit is connected correctly then the object is an insulator. You may need to test the materials before to ensure one battery will light up the bulb, or two batteries could be used instead.

Students can represent their findings in several ways such as a tick chart or labelled diagrams.

Health and safety

Hazard and risk	Precautions
Electric shock or burns from circuits.	Ensure circuit kits are used under supervision. Discard any damaged wires or bulbs. The use of batteries ensures very low voltage. Avoid handling the objects while they are being tested as they may get warm.
Broken glass from bulbs causing cuts.	Discard broken bulbs safely, immediately clear any broken glass. Use under supervision.
Objects for testing may be damaged causing cuts, or pose a choking risk.	Discard any damaged objects and avoid contact with the mouth. Use under supervision.

Adapting the activity

Extra support: students may need the circuit set up for them if they are conducting the experiment.

Extension: compare the brightness of the bulb – are some objects better conductors than others?

Optional extras: include composite materials such as crisp packets as they are made of plastic and metal. Compare where the clips are attached – does it make a difference?

Year 5 Living things and their habitats

National Curriculum Statements:

- describe the differences in the life cycles of a mammal, an amphibian, an insect and a bird;
- describe the life process of reproduction in some plants and animals.

Working scientifically:

- recording data and results of increasing complexity using scientific diagrams and labels, classification keys, tables, scatter graphs, bar and line graphs.

NC Assessment Indicators

Emerging: identify simple differences between the life cycles of mammals, amphibians and insects.

Expected: describe the differences between the life cycles of mammals, amphibians and insects.

Exceeding: suggest why differences in life cycles are necessary in different living things.

LIFE CYCLES

Equipment:

Split pin paper fasteners

Card – two pieces per students

Drawing compass OR pre-cut large circles of card OR paper plates

Scissors

Animal pictures at each stage of their life cycle, e.g. cat

Insect pictures at each stage of their life cycle, e.g. butterfly

Amphibian pictures at each stage of their life cycle, e.g. frog

Instructions:

1. Draw a large circle on the first piece of card, approximately 20 cm in diameter, and cut out. Or, use pre-cut card circles or paper plates.
2. Imagine the paper plate split into six wedge shapes, like slices of cake. Cut a window into one of the slices, following the wedge shape but not all the way to the centre.
3. On the other piece of card, draw a matching circle to the first card circle. Separate it into six wedge shaped sections using a pencil and ruler. This shape could be pre-printed onto the card if needed.
4. Place the first card circle or paper plate with the window directly over the circle drawn on to the second piece of card and secure the two with a split pin paper fastener inserted through the middle. This should allow the card on top to spin, with a little encouragement the first time to ensure the hole is large enough.
5. Starting from the top, either stick in a picture of an animal at the beginning of their life cycle, or draw the animal through the window panel. Next, rotate the top card to the next wedge section, and draw the next stage of the animal life cycle. Repeat this until all stages are complete.
6. Labels can be added to the outside edge of the back piece of card to describe each life cycle stage, e.g. new-born, adult.
7. Repeat the activity for an amphibian and an insect.

Now, the life cycle circles can be used for comparing the different stage of the life cycles of animals, amphibians and insects. Comparisons could be verbal or written.

Health and safety

Hazard and risk	Precautions
Scissors cutting students' hands, hair, clothes, etc.	Adult supervision required. Safety scissors should be used from a reputable supplier.
Compass points are sharp and cause cuts.	Adult supervision required.
Split pin paper fasteners can cause injury when piercing card.	Adult supervision required. A pilot hole can be made using the compass point before the pin is inserted.
Card or paper plate contamination.	Use only clean, new card and paper plates.

Adapting the activity

Extra support: prepare pre-printed circles with the animal pictures already present.

Extension: students can choose and research their own animal, amphibian or insect for the activity.

Optional extras: students could research the life cycles of different living things and present their findings to the class.

FLOWER DISSECTION

Check for hay fever and plant allergies, and insect stings and bite allergies before completing this activity.

Equipment:
Flowers such as alstroemeria or unopened lilies
Chopping boards
Safety scissors

Instructions:
Basic prior knowledge of flower pollination is required for this activity. This can be carried out in different ways depending on the group of students. Here is one suggested way of completing the activity.

As a group, introduce the flower and discuss what each part of the plant is for. A labelled diagram could be displayed or completed before this activity.

Each student can then take their own flower and on their chopping board, dissect the flower, separating out the stamen then further separating into the filament and anther, for example. Once the dissection is complete, the students should be able to say exactly which part is which on their chopping board.

To follow up this activity, photographs could be taken of each student's dissection, and they can then label the parts in the photograph and write a report of their experiment.

Health and safety

Hazard and risk	Precautions
Allergies to pollen, plants, flowers, insect bites or stings. Pollen may also stain if lilies are used.	Check allergies before commencing the activities. Lily pollen is a common allergen. If lilies are chosen, then they must be fresh blooms before the pollen ripens, preferably unopened buds. Alternate flowers such as alstroemeria carry less allergy risk and their pollen does not stain.
Scissors cutting students' hands, hair, clothes, etc. Contamination risk after use.	Adult supervision required. Safety scissors should be used from a reputable supplier. Scissors must be washed afterwards to prevent contamination.

Adapting the activity

Extra support: students may need a labelled flower diagram next to them to help identify the parts they find in the flower.

Extension: students can dissect various flowers and compare the parts, e.g. do all stamens look the same? Is all pollen the same colour?

Optional extras: if allergies are an issue, students can construct models of flowers from knowledge of the parts using plasticine, modelling clay, felt, card and pipe cleaners.

Year 5 Animals including humans

National Curriculum Statements:

- describe the changes as humans develop to old age.

Working scientifically:

- reporting and presenting findings from enquiries, including conclusions, causal relationships and explanations of and a degree of trust in results, in oral and written forms such as displays and other presentations.

NC Assessment Indicators

Emerging: identify some changes that occur in humans as they age.
Expected: describe the changes as humans develop to old age.
Exceeding: suggest why humans change as they age.

CHANGES AS HUMANS AGE

Equipment:
Research materials such as computer access or an information hunt around the room
A clothes hanger
String
Scissors
Sticky tape
Paper

Instructions:
Students can research the six stages of human life: foetus, baby, childhood, adolescence, adulthood, old age. Research should include the approximate ages at which these stages occur, also the main physical changes such as ability to walk, talk, etc. Puberty should be included in the research for adolescence.

Each stage can be represented as a labelled diagram and then attached with string to the clothes hanger. Attached in order, this will become a human life cycle time line!

Health and safety

Hazard and risk	Precautions
Scissors cutting students' hands, hair, clothes, etc. Contamination risk after use.	Adult supervision required. Safety scissors should be used from a reputable supplier. Scissors must be washed afterwards to prevent contamination.
Sticky tape can become wrapped around limbs.	Adult supervision required, remove immediately from limbs.

Adapting the activity

Extra support: students may need information in an easily accessible format.

Extension: include full physical changes at all stages, not just puberty.

Optional extras: students can compare the time periods such as gestation and childhood to other animals.

Year 5 Properties and changes of materials

National Curriculum Statements:

- compare and group together everyday materials on the basis of their properties, including their hardness, solubility, transparency, conductivity (electrical and thermal) and response to magnets;
- know that some materials will dissolve in liquid to form a solution, and describe how to recover a substance from a solution;
- use knowledge of solids, liquids and gases to decide how mixtures might be separated, including through filtering, sieving and evaporating;
- give reasons, based on evidence from comparative and fair tests, for the particular uses of everyday materials, including metals, wood and plastic;
- demonstrate that dissolving, mixing and changes of state are reversible changes;
- explain that some changes result in the formation of new materials, and that this kind of change is not usually reversible, including changes associated with burning and the action of acid on bicarbonate of soda.

Working scientifically:

- planning different types of scientific enquiries to answer questions, including recognising and controlling variables where necessary;
- taking measurements, using a range of scientific equipment, with increasing accuracy and precision, taking repeat readings when appropriate;
- recording data and results of increasing complexity using scientific diagrams and labels, classification keys, tables, scatter graphs, bar and line graphs;
- using test results to make predictions to set up further comparative and fair tests;

- reporting and presenting findings from enquiries, including conclusions, causal relationships and explanations of and a degree of trust in results, in oral and written forms such as displays and other presentations.

NC Assessment Indicators

Emerging: recognise that some materials will be used for certain jobs and others would not be suitable, e.g. cardboard cars would get soggy in the rain.
Expected: suggest how some mixtures may be separated, describe the common uses of some materials.
Exceeding: describe how to separate complex mixtures by recognising which materials dissolve, explain why metals have certain uses and plastics have different uses.

DISSOLVING AND SOLUTIONS

Equipment:
Sand
Salt
Flour
Pepper
Epsom salts – magnesium sulphate
Beakers or jars
Spoons
Water
Measuring cylinders
Shallow wide dishes or trays

Instructions:
Students can carry out the experiments independently or as a class led exercise. The aim is to determine whether the solid dissolves or not. Students could make predictions about each solid based on prior knowledge, or even design the experiment themselves, suggesting sensible quantities of each material.

Part 1
1. Measure out 50 cm³ of water using a measuring cylinder and pour it into a beaker.
2. Add one heaped spoonful of sand and stir for at least one minute. Observe the sand. Record whether the sand dissolves.
3. Repeat with a fresh beaker of water and a different solid. Continue until all the solids have been tested.

Sand in water and pepper in water may be saved for further experiments.

Part 2

Once a solid has dissolved into a solution, it can be recovered! If there is access to a cooking room, then salt water can be gently heated as a demonstration only, removing the majority of the water and leaving a salt crust on the saucepan. This can be quite tricky, and a risk assessment must be carried out.

Alternatively, take the solution of salt water and continue to add salt to it, stirring in at least two more heaped spoonfuls of salt. This should ensure the solution is saturated. Pour the solution into a large shallow dish or tray, and place on a warm windowsill or other suitable place. Over time, the water will evaporate and leave behind the salt. Large salt crystals can form and are square when formed slowly.

Repeat this with the Epsom salt solution, adding two more spoonfuls of Epsom salts to the water and stirring well. Again, pour into a large shallow dish and leave to evaporate. If the solution is slow to evaporate, add a small amount of fabric such as a piece of dishcloth to stimulate crystal formation. Magnesium sulphate crystals can be very spiky.

Health and safety

Hazard and risk	Precautions
Solids – sand, salt, flour, pepper, Epsom salts can cause irritation and danger if swallowed.	Adult supervision required. None of the solids or solutions should be tasted or ingested.
Water spillages can be a slipping hazard.and water is a contamination risk if consumed.	Clear any spillages immediately. The water should not be drunk at any time.
Beakers and measuring cylinders can smash and cause cuts.	If using glass beakers, goggles may be worn to protect against glass shards. If beakers are plastic, then goggles do not have to be worn. Measuring cylinders should be plastic and discarded if damaged.
Spoons – contamination risk.	Spoons should be thoroughly washed after use and not used for food.
Evaporating the water from a solution in a warm place such as a windowsill – risk of spillage or accidental consumption.	Solutions should not be left within reach of students and should be clearly labelled as a warning for staff. Ensure solutions are placed in an area where they are unlikely to be disturbed to reduce risk of spillages. Clear any spillages immediately to prevent slipping.

Adapting the activity

Extra support: students may need to discuss what a dissolved solution would look like, the idea that the solid will 'disappear' from sight, but it is still present in the solution.

Extension: try dissolving other substances such as wax, soap or jelly. Predictions may again be made based on students' prior knowledge or logical reasoning.

Optional extras: students can compare how the temperature of the water affects the rate at which solids dissolve, e.g. ice-cold water and hot water.

SEPARATING MIXTURES

Equipment:
Mixture 1 – sand and paper clips
Mixture 2 – sand in water
Mixture 3 – sand and marbles
Mixture 4 – cooking oil and water
Sieve
Filter paper and funnel
Magnets
Jugs
Beakers

Instructions:
Give students samples of all of mixtures and access to all of the equipment. Students can choose which pieces of equipment to use to separate the mixtures and test their theories.

As a guide, mixture 1 can be separated by using a magnet or sieving out the paper clips from the sand.

Mixture 2 can be filtered using a funnel and filter paper – this is a slow process.

Mixture 3 can be separated using a sieve or even by hand.

Mixture 4 can be separated by carefully pouring off the oil.

Health and safety

Hazard and risk	Precautions
Mixtures pose a contamination and choking hazard. Spillages can cause slips and trips.	Adult supervision required. None of the mixtures should be put near the mouth or consumed. Any spillages should be cleared immediately.

Hazard and risk	Precautions
Magnets can affect medical implants and trap flesh.	Check medical information for students and staff. Use only standard school blue and red magnets which should not be strong enough to trap skin.
Beakers and jugs can smash and cause cuts.	If using glass beakers, goggles may be worn to protect against glass shards. If beakers are plastic, then goggles do not have to be worn. Jugs should be plastic and discarded if damaged.
Filter paper, funnels and sieves – contamination risk.	Use under supervision. Filter paper is single use. Funnels should be thoroughly washed after use and avoid contact with the mouth. Sieves should only be used for science experiments and not food preparation.

Adapting the activity

Extra support: students may need to handle the mixtures to explore the different materials in each one. Give students only one mixture at a time to investigate.

Extension: try more complex mixtures like sand and salt, where a combination of techniques are necessary.

Optional extras: students can discover how liquids can also be mixtures by carrying out felt tip pen chromatography.

TESTING USES OF MATERIALS

Equipment:

Metal teaspoon

Wooden teaspoon – alternatively use wooden craft sticks

Plastic spoon – similar size to metal spoon

Metal, wooden and plastic rulers

Cardboard strips the same size as the rulers

Small masses

Access to hot water

Petroleum jelly

Drawing pin or paper clip

Scales

Two clamp stands, clamps and bosses

Instructions:

These tests can be carried out on separate occasions or in continuously to examine the uses of everyday materials. The tests should stimulate discussion about the uses of the materials. Students can plan the experiments or discuss how to make them fair tests for comparisons.

Test 1: strength test
Clamp the wooden ruler on either end, raised above the table to allow room for testing.

Carefully place a mass in the middle of the ruler. Observe the wooden ruler. Does it bend? Continue adding masses until the wooden ruler bends – try to avoid overloading and snapping the ruler.

Repeat the experiment with the cardboard strip, the plastic ruler and the metal ruler.

Consider why large bridges or skyscrapers are made out of metal.

Test 2: heat conductor
Place the three types of spoon into beaker. If students notice a difference in size between the spoons, try to use alternatives of similar sizes, e.g. wooden craft sticks are approximately the same size as a metal teaspoon.

Using petroleum jelly, stick a drawing pin or paper clip to the end of the spoons.

Pour hot water into the beaker and observe the order in which the petroleum jelly melts and the pins drop off.

The best conductor of heat will transit the heat energy to the petroleum jelly first.

Consider why we use metal saucepans, but wooden or plastic handles based on the results of this experiment.

Test 3: mass of each spoon
Spoons need to be of similar sizes for this test.

Place each spoon on scales and record their mass. Consider how the mass affects the uses of the material, e.g. would you make a carrier bag out of metal? What would happen if you made gates and fences out of plastic?

Wooden and plastic building blocks of the same sizes can also be weighed and compared.

Health and safety

Hazard and risk	Precautions
Spoons, rulers, cardboard strips, drawing pins and beakers.	Adult supervision required. The items can bend, snap and splinter or shatter. Discard items if they are damaged. Add masses slowly to avoid overloading and snapping materials.
Hot water could scald students and staff, spillages can be a slipping hazard.	Hot water should be poured by staff only – avoid using boiling water. Any spillages should be cleared immediately.
Petroleum jelly.	Use under supervision. Petroleum jelly used for experiments should not be used for other purposes. Keep away from flames.
Scales – electronic scales can risk electrocution.	Use under supervision and away from water.
Clamp stands clamps and bosses may fall on students or staff.	Use away from the edge of the table, use under supervision.

Adapting the activity

Extra support: conduct experiments as demonstrations with smaller groups of students. A thermometer could be included to help indicate how hot the water is.

Extension: try bending materials by hand to test how malleable the materials are – be aware the wooden spoon or wooden craft sticks could splinter.

Optional extras: students can suggest ridiculous uses for everyday materials, e.g. a chocolate teapot would melt, a wooden frying pan would burn, a plastic BBQ would melt.

MATERIALS FOR INSULATION

Equipment:
Beakers
Ice cubes
Timers or stop clocks
Various materials including fabric, foil, bubble wrap, cotton wool, paper
Elastic bands
Scissors

Instructions:
The aim of this experiment is to keep the ice cubes cold! Students may have the misconception that wrapping a beaker in material will make the ice cube warm, like wearing a coat keeps them warm, as they will not understand how heat is transferred yet. One way of explaining insulation is to consider a cool bag with their sandwiches in – the thick bag does not warm their sandwiches, but stops heat getting in to them.

Students can complete this experiment on their own or in small groups.

1. Wrap a beaker in a chosen material. Use an elastic band to secure the material onto the beaker.
2. Place two ice cubes into the beaker and start the timer.
3. Every two minutes, check the ice cubes to see if they have melted.
4. When the ice has completely melted, stop the timer and record the time.

Students can share results for different materials and plot their results in a bar chart before drawing a conclusion on common materials that are good insulators. Do not forget to include one unwrapped beaker as a control.

Health and safety

Hazard and risk	Precautions
Beakers can shatter and cause cuts.	Adult supervision required. Discard items if they are damaged. Consider plastic beakers instead of glass beakers if concerned about breakages.
Ice cubes can cause cold burns and melt causing a slipping hazard.	Ice cubes should not be handled for more than a few seconds. Any spillages should be cleared immediately.
Elastic bands and materials can snap and be flicked at students.	Use under supervision. Hand out elastic bands as needed. Monitor how much foil and how many elastic bands are handed out to students to lessen wastage and the possibility of them being thrown or flicked.
Stop clocks or timers.	Use under supervision. Ensure timers have undamaged batteries and the batteries are sufficiently sealed to prevent students taking them out easily.
Scales – electronic scales can risk electrocution.	Use under supervision and away from water.
Clamp stands, clamps and bosses may fall on students or staff.	Use away from the edge of the table, use under supervision.

Adapting the activity

Extra support: students could have three beakers in front of them, one unwrapped and two wrapped in different materials, each with one ice cube in, and observe the changes without recording the time.

Extension: students could record the temperature over time using $0°C$ as the end-point for the experiment.

Optional extras: consider what would make the test fair, for example do the beakers need lids? Should the bottom of the beaker be wrapped too?

REVERSIBLE AND IRREVERSIBLE CHANGES

Equipment:

Vinegar

Bicarbonate of soda

Beakers

Salt

Water

Small chocolates in wrappers or ice cubes

A raw lion stamped egg

A cooking method for the egg – microwave OR a raw egg and a cooked egg

Kettle

Matches

Burnt toast and slice of bread

Teaspoons

Goggles or safety glasses

Instructions:

Students can carry out some of the experiments, but the matches and boiling kettle should be demonstrations only. The cooked egg, raw egg, burnt toast and slice of bread are for observation only and should not be passed around the room.

Experiment 1

1. Place two teaspoons of bicarbonate of soda into a beaker.
2. Add a generous splash of vinegar – amount is not important if there is enough for a fizzing reaction.
3. Record observations.
4. Answer the question 'can it be reversed?'

Experiment 2

1. Half fill a beaker with water.
2. Add two teaspoons of salt and stir.
3. Record observations – what happened to the salt?
4. Answer the question 'can it be reversed?'

Experiment 3

1. Hold a chocolate in a wrapper in the hands. Feel the shape and hardness.
2. Continue holding. Check the shape and hardness. What happens?
3. Record the observations. Answer the question 'can it be reversed?'

Demonstrations

Students can observe a kettle boiling. What happens? Answer the question 'can it be reversed?'

Students should watch the teacher light a match then examine the used match when cooled. What has happened to it? Can it be reversed?

Allow students to visually observe the raw egg and the cooked egg, then the bread and the burnt toast. What happened to each of these? Can they be reversed?

As a guide
Vinegar and bicarbonate of soda – irreversible
Salt dissolving in water – reversible
Chocolate in wrappers melt in hands (or ice cubes) – reversible
Raw egg to cooked egg – irreversible
Bread to burnt toast – irreversible
Kettle boiling water – reversible
Light a match – irreversible.

Health and safety

Hazard and risk	Precautions
Beakers can shatter and cause cuts.	Adult supervision required. Discard items if they are damaged. Consider plastic beakers instead of glass beakers if concerned about breakages.
Ice cubes can cause cold burns and melt to form water, causing a slipping hazard.	Ice cubes should not be handled for more than a few seconds in each hand before swapping hand. Any spillages should be cleared immediately.
Foods including eggs, bread and chocolate can cause allergies and contamination can cause illness.	Use under supervision. Eggs should be lion stamped to prevent salmonella transmission and should not be handled by students. Allergies should be checked before the activity commences. No food should be consumed once used in experiments.
Vinegar bicarbonate of soda and salt can be spilt and cause a slipping hazard. Can also sting damaged skin. Chemicals can be splashed in eyes.	Use under supervision. Goggles or safety glasses are recommended to prevent any chemicals in the eye. If this occurs, rinse well with water. Medical advice should be sought if the person is still in distress after rinsing. None of the chemical should be consumed. Any spillages should be cleared immediately.
Kettles and matches can cause burns or scalds.	Used by staff only, out of the reach of children. Matches should be disposed of in a sensible manner as hot matches can cause fires. Ensure a fire bucket or fire blanket is on hand for this demonstration.

Adapting the activity

Extra support: if a cooking room is available, small groups of students can observe bread becoming toast or eggs frying to see the changes that take place.

Extension: can students think of other irreversible changes? E.g. cake mixtures becoming a cake.

Optional extras: the water can be evaporated from the salt water mixture to reveal the salt, proving that it was a reversible change.

Year 5 Earth and space

The activities here enhance learning of the solar system but cannot be used alone.

MODEL SOLAR SYSTEM

Equipment:
String
Kebab sticks or thin wooden dowels
Small polystyrene ball
Sharp scissors
Hot glue
Planet and Sun shapes – pre-prepared, coloured or printed and labelled

Instructions:
Start by attaching the string to the small polystyrene ball with hot glue, in a long loop to hang the mobile.

Directly underneath, glue on a length of string with the Sun picture attached. This is the centre of the mobile and solar system!

Take a short piece of wooden dowel, approximately 7 cm in length and insert it onto the polystyrene ball so it is horizontal. Make sure at least 2 cm of the stick is inside the polystyrene ball, and glue it into place.

Attach a piece of string to the end of the stick and suspend Mercury. This is closest to the Sun.

Now take a stick of length 8 cm and repeat the process, sticking it into the polystyrene ball 1 cm or so further along than the first stick. Again, glue it into place and this time suspend Venus using string.

Repeat the steps with sticks of lengths 9 cm, 11 cm, 20 cm, 23 cm, 27 cm and 30 cm apart, with the remaining planets attached in order from Earth to Neptune.

The mobile should spin freely on the string, so the planets can model orbiting the Sun, with the Sun remaining underneath the polystyrene ball.

Health and safety

Hazard and risk	Precautions
Scissors cutting students' hands, hair, clothing, etc.	Adult supervision required. Safety scissors should be used from a reputable supplier.
String can be a tripping hazard or get wrapped around limbs or the neck posing a strangulation risk.	Use under supervision. Short lengths of string should be used to reduce risk of it wrapping around limbs, etc. Alternatively, use easy snap wool instead of string so it can easily be removed from a child's limbs or neck.
Hot glue guns can cause burns from the glue and the metal tip of the glue gun.	Use under supervision or appoint an adult to operate the glue gun. Cool melt glue guns can be purchased which heat the glue to a lower temperature reducing the risk of burns from the glue.
Kebab sticks or wooden dowel can splinter and cause cuts or have sharp edges which can stab flesh or eyes.	Inspect items for damage and discard if necessary. Use hot glue to cover any ends of kebab sticks or dowel which may be considered sharp.

Adapting the activity

Extra support: provide pictures of planets to begin with, or construct the basic model leaving students to attach the planets in the right order. This could be done on a larger scale so a classroom sized model is produced.

Extension: students can use various internet resources to plan the distances between the planets and the Sun to scale for their model!

Optional extras: students could research the names and order of the planets before the activity, possibly even drawing their own planet pictures to a sensible scale for their planet mobile. Planets can even be constructed out of further polystyrene balls, matching the size of the ball to the planet to ensure a similar representation of size differences.

THE EARTH AND THE MOON

Equipment:
A large space
Students and staff

Instructions:
To demonstrate that the Earth only ever sees one face or side of the Moon, even though the Moon orbits the Earth, organise this physical modelling activity to take place. It can be done in small groups or as a class.

Assign a volunteer to represent the Moon.

Assign six volunteers to represent the Earth. They must stand in a circle, linking arms but facing outwards.

First the Earth can remain still and the Moon slowly walks around the Earth by stepping sideways, making sure to face the Earth the whole way around.

The audience should see that the Moon has made one full turn as well as going around the Earth once.

The Earth volunteers can confirm that the Moon faced them the whole time, so they have only seen the front face of the Moon.

Make the physical modelling a little trickier but more realistic by asking the Earth to also rotate, stepping sideways to make the planet 'spin'. The Moon should walk a lot slower than the Earth as it orbits the Earth. Again, the Earth will only see the front face of the Moon despite the Moon making one full rotation.

If students are not sure that the Moon actually has rotated on its axis, demonstrate the Moon's movements without the Earth, so that everyone can see the Moon does in fact turn around once.

Health and safety

Hazard and risk	Precautions
Tripping and slipping in area.	Remove all trip hazards, use a large space to allow movement without bumping into each other or furniture.

Adapting the activity

Extra support: demonstrate this with adults first, then in small groups of students, prompting the observations as the activity continues.

Extension: students can be specific about the number of rotations of the Earth for each rotation of the Moon and link it to the length of a month.

Optional extras: for a bit of fun, stick an animal picture on the back of the Moon, and ask the Earth if they know what the picture is. They will not know, because they will not be able to see the back of the Moon.

Year 5 Forces

National Curriculum Statements:

- explain that unsupported objects fall towards the Earth because of the force of gravity acting between the Earth and the falling object;
- identify the effects of air resistance, water resistance and friction that act between moving surfaces.

Working scientifically:

- planning different types of scientific enquiries to answer questions, including recognising and controlling variables where necessary;
- taking measurements, using a range of scientific equipment, with increasing accuracy and precision, taking repeat readings when appropriate;
- recording data and results of increasing complexity using scientific diagrams and labels, classification keys, tables, scatter graphs, bar and line graphs.

NC Assessment Indicators

Emerging: recognition of gravity acting on objects.

Expected: describe the effects of air resistance, water resistance and friction acting on objects.

Exceeding: suggest how forces can be useful, or how they can be overcome.

EGG DROP CHALLENGE

Equipment:
Raw eggs, lion stamped
String
Small plastic sheets, e.g. cut up bin liners
Large bin liner or shower curtain or plastic table cloth

Newspaper
Scissors
Sticky tape

Instructions:
This can be carried out as an activity in small groups, bringing the students back together for testing at the end.

Pose the question 'what happens when we drop an egg?' to establish that gravity will cause an object to fall towards the ground. Gravity can be tested simply by jumping up and down.

The next question is 'how can a skydiver jump out of an aeroplane and land safely?' to stimulate discussion.

Students have access to the materials listed above to make something that will allow the egg to land safely when dropped, and one simple rule – the egg which is acting as a stand in for a skydiver cannot be completely covered.

Health and safety

Hazard and risk	Precautions
Scissors cutting students' hands, hair, clothing, etc.	Adult supervision required. Safety scissors should be used from a reputable supplier.
Raw eggs can transmit salmonella and cause allergies.	Check allergies before using raw eggs. Use only lion stamped eggs as they are immunised against salmonella.
Sticky tape can become wrapped around limbs.	Adult supervision required, remove immediately from limbs.
Plastic bin bags can cause suffocation.	Use under supervision. Plastic should never be placed over the face.
Newspaper can contain offensive material.	Use only reputable newspaper brands and check the contents before using.
String can be a tripping hazard or get wrapped around limbs or the neck posing a strangulation risk.	Use under supervision. Short lengths of string should be used to reduce risk of it wrapping around limbs, etc. Alternatively, use easy snap wool instead of string so it can easily be removed from a child's limbs or neck.

Adapting the activity
Extra support: show students picture of sky divers, aeroplanes, gliders, birds and even seeds that are dispersed by the wind. These can stimulate ideas in the students.

Extension: the materials could be rationed for each group or each material given a cost, with extra challenge of being the cheapest method that protects the egg when it is dropped.

Optional extras: drop the egg from a first floor window for extra testing!

HOMEMADE FRICTION BOARDS

Equipment:
Five lengths of thick corrugated cardboard – any size above A4 is fine
An old towel or tea towel
Cling film
Foil
Sand paper
Glue
Bulldog clips
Toy cars
Tape measures
Timers or stop clocks

Instructions:
Set up: keep one cardboard length as it is. Cover one of the boards in cling film, keeping it as stretched and smooth as possible. Cover another board in foil, again keeping it smooth and flat. Glue sandpaper across the other board, taking care to minimise the effect of join lines. Using bulldog clips, attach the towel or tea towel across the final piece of card. You now have a set of friction boards!

There are two ways to use the friction boards.

Method 1
1. Raise the friction board on a ramp of books. Use the same height ramp each time.
2. Place a toy car at the top of the ramp. Start the timer and release the car.
3. Stop the timer when the car reaches the bottom of the ramp.
4. Repeat with all friction boards.

Method 2
1. Raise the friction board on a ramp of books. Use the same height ramp each time.
2. Place a toy car at the top of the ramp and gently release the car.
3. Measure the distance the car travels from the top of the ramp to where the car stops
4. Repeat with all friction boards.

Results can be displayed as bar charts, then conclusions drawn from the results. Which surface allowed the car to travel the fastest or furthest? Which surface had the least friction? How does friction affect the speed of an object?

Health and safety

Hazard and risk	Precautions
Cardboard friction boards can be trip hazard or have sharp edges.	These should be prepared for the students to use, without any sharp edges.
Toy cars are a tripping and slipping hazard.	The activity needs to be carried out in a large area to reduce the likelihood of stepping on the toy cars. Toy cars must be picked up once the experiments are finished.
Timers or stop clocks.	Use under supervision. Ensure timers have undamaged batteries and the batteries are sufficiently sealed to prevent students taking them out easily.
Measuring tapes can wrap around limbs or be a tripping hazard.	Use under supervision. Measuring tapes should be used flat on the floor to minimise risk of tripping over.

Adapting the activity

Extra support: cut the boards into thin strips wide enough for a toy car and stick cardboard strips down the edges as barriers to prevent the cars coming off the boards mid-way down.

Extension: repeat three times to get an average. Try other coverings for the friction boards too.

Optional extras: try other objects down the ramps to investigate friction between two different types of surfaces, e.g. a shoe, a smooth CD.

CATAPULTS

Equipment:
Wooden craft sticks
Hot glue
Elastic bands
Wooden teaspoons
Small polystyrene balls or small lumps of plasticine

Instructions:
Stack the wooden craft sticks into a square shape with the ends overlapping and glue into place. Add two more layers to the sticks to ensure a stable base.

Wrap an elastic band around the wooden base so it crosses over the square base like a belt in the middle.

Take the handle of a wooden teaspoon and place it through the gap between the front and back of the elastic band, in the middle of the base.

Now twist the spoon in the elastic band to store energy. The spoon should now act as a lever to catapult an object. If the concave face of the spoon is facing the wrong way, simply turn it around inside the elastic band.

Now a small force from the finger becomes a larger force using the lever, flinging a ball of plasticine much further than just flicking it by hand. To increase the force, add more twists to the elastic band.

Health and safety

Hazard and risk	Precautions
Small polystyrene balls and plasticine can be choking hazards and tripping and slipping hazards.	Use under supervision. All parts should be picked up off the floor once used to prevent tripping and slipping. No parts should be placed in or near the mouth.
Hot glue guns can cause burns from the hot glue or the metal tip.	Use under supervision or appoint an adult to operate the glue gun. Cool melt glue guns can be purchased which heat the glue to a lower temperature reducing the risk of burns from the glue.
Wooden craft sticks and teaspoons can snap and splinter.	Use under supervision. Discard any damaged sticks.
Elastic bands.	Use under supervision. Hand out elastic bands as needed. Monitor how many elastic bands are handed out to students to lesson wastage and the possibility of them being thrown or flicked.

Adapting the activity
Extra support: prepare the wooden bases by gluing the craft sticks together ready for students.
Extension: can a release mechanism be added using string?
Optional extras: make a target out of tissue paper in a cardboard frame. The extra force from the level mechanism and stored elastic energy should be enough to break through the tissue paper.

Year 6 Living things and their habitats

National Curriculum Statements:

- describe how living things are classified into broad groups according to common observable characteristics and based on similarities and differences, including micro-organisms, plants and animals;
- give reasons for classifying plants and animals based on specific characteristics.

Working scientifically:

- recording data and results of increasing complexity using scientific diagrams and labels, classification keys, tables, scatter graphs, bar and line graphs;
- identifying scientific evidence that has been used to support or refute ideas or arguments.

NC Assessment Indicators

Emerging: identify vertebrate groups such as fish, reptiles, amphibians, etc.
Expected: describe the common characteristics of vertebrate and invertebrate groups.
Exceeding: suggest why it is useful to classify animals and plants.

CLASSIFYING ANIMALS

Equipment:

A set of cards with picture of animals on including:

Mammals – cats, humans, cows, sheep, elephants, giraffes, dolphins, whales, etc.

Birds – penguins, emus, blackbirds, robins, owls, etc.

Fish – cod, goldfish, clown fish, sharks, etc.

Amphibians – newts, frogs, toads, etc.

Reptiles – snakes, alligators, lizards, etc.
Mixed invertebrate pictures including examples of all groups

Instructions:
In small groups, give students packs of the pictures. Ask them to sort them into groups of their choice, but they must justify it.

Use prompt questions to help them group into the five vertebrate groups, e.g. what features make an animal a bird? What features make a fish a fish? What is the difference between an amphibian and a reptile?

Once students have sorted the cards into the five vertebrate groups, they can represent the features of those five groups in labelled diagrams or even Venn diagrams where features cross over, e.g. scales on the skin.

Now, ask students the difference between a crab and a fish, or a worm and a sheep. Try and elicit that vertebrates have backbones, but invertebrates do not. Explain that even invertebrates can be classified again! Give students the definitions for the different invertebrate groups and allow them to sort the cards into those groups.

Adapting the activity
Extra support: reduce the number of vertebrate examples down to one each to begin with, slowly adding more examples that students can identify using the examples they have already identified as birds, fish, etc.
Extension: conduct an invertebrate hunt (bug hunt) using classification keys and keep a tally of how many of each type are identified outside the classroom. Introduce the confusion surrounding the classification of the platypus when it was first discovered.
Optional extras: demonstrate the difference between vertebrates and invertebrates by dissecting a crab and a fish to reveal the backbone only in the fish.

Year 6 Animals including humans

National Curriculum Statements:

- identify and name the main parts of the human circulatory system, and describe the functions of the heart, blood vessels and blood;
- recognise the impact of diet, exercise, drugs and lifestyle on the way their bodies function;
- describe the ways in which nutrients and water are transported within animals, including humans.

Working scientifically:

- recording data and results of increasing complexity using scientific diagrams and labels, classification keys, tables, scatter graphs, bar and line graphs;
- reporting and presenting findings from enquiries, including conclusions, causal relationships and explanations of and a degree of trust in results, in oral and written forms such as displays and other presentations.

NC Assessment Indicators

Emerging: identify some parts of the human circulatory system.
Expected: describe functions of parts of the circulatory system, and how nutrients and water are transported in animals including humans. Suggest how lifestyle can impact the function of the body.
Exceeding: explain how diet, exercise, drugs and lifestyle can affect the function of the body.

MODEL OF THE BLOOD

Equipment:
Jars with lids
Cooking oil or glycerin

Red sweets such as Skittles, Millions or similar
White mints such as mint imperials
Cereal or jazzies type sweets

Instructions:
Start by asking pupils what they think the blood is made of. This may lead to questions about the blood such as its colour.

The main constituent of blood is in fact plasma, a yellowish liquid that carries all of the blood cells and chemicals around the body in the blood vessels. The cooking oil or glycerin can represent this. Fill the jar at ¾ full of cooking oil or glycerin.

Next add a few white mints that represent white blood cells, approximately four for a standard jam jar sized model. These white blood cells fight infections and keep the human body healthy.

Red blood cells carry oxygen and can be represented by red sweets. There should be at least three times as many red blood cells as white cells in the model, although in reality there are far more red blood cells than white blood cells.

Platelets are a vital part of blood that form clots and prevent continuous bleeding. These are made from large cells that shatter into pieces. Take the jazzies type sweets or cereal flakes and snap them into large irregular pieces and add them to the model. Approximately three large flakes are suitable for this model.

Place the lid on the jar, then give it a gentle shake. The overall colour should be red although there may be an excess of cooking oil.

Health and safety

Hazard and risk	Precautions
Glass jars may smash and cause cuts.	Use under supervision. Clear any damaged or smashed glass immediately.
Cooking oil, glycerin, sweets and cereal pose a contamination risk if consumed, and may cause allergies.	Check allergies before commencing this activity. No parts of the model should be consumed before or after use.

Adapting the activity
Extra support: put the ingredients in dishes labelled as white blood cells, red blood cells and platelets.

Extension: research the actual amounts of each constituent of the blood and create an accurate (although not as interesting) model.

Optional extras: consider how other chemicals carried in the blood could be represented, e.g. carbon dioxide.

MODEL OF THE BLOOD VESSELS

Equipment:

Cardboard tubes such as those in the centre of toilet rolls or kitchen rolls

Thick pipe lagging with thin diameter opening, cut into small lengths

Red card or paper

White card or paper

Paper art straws

Glue

Scissors

Instructions:

Students will need to research the difference in blood vessels before this activity, then using the information they have collected they can build models of each of the three types of blood vessels using the supplies offered to them.

As a guide, thick pipe lagging with a small diameter opening can be used as arteries representing thick muscular walls.

Veins can be represented using the cardboard tubes, with added valves using paper or straws.

Paper art straws make excellent capillaries as they are very thin and small compared to other models.

Health and safety

Hazard and risk	Precautions
Scissors cutting students' hands, hair, clothes, etc.	Adult supervision required. Safety scissors should be used from a reputable supplier.
Glue can get stuck to skin, hair and clothes.	Use only glue sticks or PVA glue from a school supplier.
Cardboard tubes, pipe lagging and paper may be contaminated.	Ensure the items are clean and wash hands after using.

Adapting the activity

Extra support: offer students a picture representation of the three types of blood vessel.

Extension: consider how the blood vessels are connected in the body and connect them, e.g. arteries connect to capillaries, which then connect to veins.

Optional extras: include a representation of blood in the blood vessels, or produce an information sheet to go with the models.

HEART DISSECTION

This activity uses food grade animal parts, which could cause discomfort for students that are vegetarian or vegan, or those with eating disorders or sensitivities over food. Students should be offered the chance to observe instead of handling the hearts themselves. Some students may object to the practical and should be offered an alternate activity.

Equipment:
Sheep or pigs' hearts – these can be ordered from online suppliers for schools, butchers or even supermarkets
Chopping boards
Safety scissors or dissection scissors
Single use gloves – preferably latex free

Instructions:
Students will need to have basic knowledge of the function of the heart, and the major parts of the heart. The dissections can be done in pairs or threes, or teacher led small groups. If dissection scissors are not available, safety scissors can be used and sterilised afterwards.

Students and staff should wear gloves and avoid touching their faces, hair or clothes once they handle a heart. A heart can be opened by cutting down the sides of the heart, then through the septum to separate it into two halves. There are many videos available online to demonstrate how to do this if staff have not had experience or would like to refresh their memory.

Students can identify that the heart has four chambers, that there are valves in the heart and even determine which blood vessels are which by stretching and feeling them.

After the activity, students can record their observations in a written report or even include diagrams of what they did.

Health and safety

Hazard and risk	Precautions
Scissors cutting students' hands, hair, clothes, etc.	Adult supervision required. Safety scissors should be used from a reputable supplier, or dissection scissors. If concerns over motor control, safety scissors are safer. Sterilise the scissors after use.
Animal hearts can be a contamination risk.	Use only food grade hearts and treat as raw meat. Sterilise benches and all equipment after use, wear gloves when handling the heart and wash hands with soap after the experiment.
Single use gloves.	Dispose of carefully after use. Check allergies before commencing activity – latex free or hypoallergenic gloves may be required.

Adapting the activity

Extra support: offer students an alternate activity to dissecting a real heart. Present them with a picture or watch a video to show them the parts of the heart so they can recognise them during the dissection.

Extension: compare the size of the hearts dissected to those of humans. Can students name parts of the heart?

Optional extras: order a pluck to show the location of the heart within the chest cavity. Take photographs of the activity to complement the report writing.

LIFESTYLE AND BODY FUNCTIONS

Equipment:

Information sheets on the effects of drugs, alcohol, exercise and fatty foods on the body

Pens, paper, pencils – project materials

Instructions:

This can be a difficult topic to teach as students may have traumatic experiences of these factors within their family. The other issue with teaching this topic is it can be predominantly teacher led which can make concentration difficult.

Students could complete an information hunt on the lifestyle factors and produce a presentation, comic strip or project on the information they have found.

Alternatively, students could conduct the research themselves using student friendly websites.

This can take place over several lessons.

Health and safety

Hazard and risk	Precautions
Information sheets may cause emotional distress.	Check known history of pupils before commencing the activity. A sensitive approach is required as students may have family members with lifestyle issues, or have body issues of their own.
Inappropriate internet sites causing emotional stress.	Carefully select age appropriate internet sites – check all pages before allowing access.
Paper cuts.	Discard any dirty materials. Paper needs to be in good condition and clean for use in the classroom.

Adapting the activity

Extra support: offer students a choice over which lifestyle factor to research.

Extension: include the impact on life as well as body function for diet, drugs, exercise, etc., e.g. diet can affect the body by fat clogging arteries. This can lead to heart attacks, this might mean a person can no longer go to work.

Optional extras: in conclusion to the activity, students could produce a healthy living guide, advising how best to limit damage to body function from the lifestyle factors researched.

Year 6 Evolution and inheritance

National Curriculum Statements:

- recognise that living things have changed over time and that fossils provide information about living things that inhabited the Earth millions of years ago;
- recognise that living things produce offspring of the same kind, but normally offspring vary and are not identical to their parents;
- identify how animals and plants are adapted to suit their environment in different ways and that adaptation may lead to evolution.

Working scientifically:

- recording data and results of increasing complexity using scientific diagrams and labels, classification keys, tables, scatter graphs, bar and line graphs;
- reporting and presenting findings from enquiries, including conclusions, causal relationships and explanations of and a degree of trust in results, in oral and written forms such as displays and other presentations;
- identifying scientific evidence that has been used to support or refute ideas or arguments.

NC Assessment Indicators

Emerging: recognise that living things change over time.
Expected: recognise that living things produce offspring. Describe how animals and plants are adapted to suit their environment.
Exceeding: suggest why animals need to be adapted to their environments.

GIRAFFES THEN AND NOW!

Equipment:
Pictures of ancient giraffes/giraffe ancestors and modern giraffes

Instructions:
This is a comparative activity. Students can have both pictures on a page and circle any differences, like a spot the difference game.

This can then stimulate discussion. Here are some prompt questions:

How have the giraffes changed? Why did the giraffes change?

How quickly did they change?

Was a giraffe suddenly born looking like a modern giraffe?

Adapting the activity
Extra support: the activity could be group discussion rather than individual writing.
Extension: include pictures of several giraffe ancestors, so changes can be identified over time. Show an evolution tree for the giraffes or other animals and ask why we do not see modern versions of all of those animals today.
Optional extras: compare modern elephants to their ancestors, or modern horses to ancient horses.

DINOSAURS

Equipment:
Pictures of dinosaurs or plastic dinosaurs
Fossil pictures showing the bones or even footprints of each dinosaur

Instructions:
Match the dinosaurs to the fossils. How do we know which dinosaur is which? Look at the skeleton in the fossils, observe the leg lengths, how many legs they are walking on, jaw size, etc.

Adapting the activity
Extra support: only use pictures of skeletons to match to the dinosaurs. Include some obviously different dinosaurs, e.g. marine dinosaurs and flying dinosaurs.
Extension: revisit the activity on fossils from Year 3 to remind students how fossils are made.
Optional extras: look at the work of Mary Anning on fossils.

PARENT AND OFFSPRING

Equipment:
Parent and offspring pictures printed on cards or pieces of paper, e.g. cat and kitten, butterfly and caterpillar, tadpole and frog, foal and horse, etc.
A picture of a cat and its litter of kittens – choose one that shows the most variation between the mother and the offspring

Instructions:
Begin with matching the parent and the offspring. This could be a simple card game in small groups or a whole class task with the cards placed around the room for students to find, then a wall space for them to stick the cards in matching pairs.

Once it is established that animals have offspring of the same type, variation can be considered. Show the picture of the cat with the kittens. Ask for observations on the pictures – what do students notice about the kittens? Do they all look the same? Do they all look like the mother cat?

Establish that offspring vary and are not identical to their parents. Link it to identical twins looking like each other but normal sibling groups not having as many similarities.

Adapting the activity
Extra support: topics dealing with parents and offspring can be difficult for some students – be aware of their personal situation and guide discussions with respect to their circumstances.
Extension: students do not need to know about genes and chromosomes at this stage, but DNA can be mentioned – DNA coming from both parents giving variation. Students can research basic information on DNA.
Optional extras: consider dog breeds – how do you get a labradoodle? Consider characteristics passed from both parents causing the offspring to look different.

ADAPTATIONS!

Equipment:
Pictures of animals and plants with no background graphics, printed on paper for students
Corresponding animals and plants in their habitats as a PowerPoint, etc. for the board
Tracing paper
Stapler

Instructions:

First consider the polar bear. Give students a picture of a polar bear and ask them what the habitat would look like. Use pictures on the board to help students consider the local environment and draw it around the polar bear.

Now staple a sheet of tracing paper over the student's pictures. On this page the adaptations can be considered and annotated on to make a flip booklet of the adaptations and then the polar bear in its habitat.

Repeat the activity with a camel in the desert, a cactus in the desert and even seaweed in the sea!

Adaptations as a guide:
How can a polar bear walk in the snow and not sink? Look at the feet!

How can the polar bear walk around on ice and not freeze? Look at the fur and fat layer.

How can the polar bear catch and eat seals? Look at the teeth.

How can a camel walk in the sand without sinking? Look at the feet.

How can a camel travel without food? Look at the fat store in the hump.

How can a camel see in a sand storm? Look at the eyes.

How can a cactus survive without much water? Look at the roots.

How can a cactus prevent its leaves being eaten by animals? Look at the spines.

How can a seaweed make sure it's leaves can get sunlight? Look at the bladders on bladder wrack!

Health and safety

Hazard and risk	Precautions
Stapler and staples can cause cuts.	Stapler should be used by adults, ensure there are no sharp edges on stapled sheets.
Tracing paper can cause paper cuts.	Use clean paper for this project.

Adapting the activity

Extra support: students can begin with a picture of the animal in its habitat already.

Extension: suggest what would happen to a polar bear in a desert, or a camel in the arctic.

Optional extras: consider the differences between black bears and polar bears or grizzly bears and polar bears. How did they become so different? Link the differences to the ability to survive in their environments.

Year 6 Light

SHADOWS

Equipment:
Torch
Objects with various shapes
Kebab sticks with blu tack on the ends

Instructions:
Place an object on a table in front of the wall.

Use kebab sticks with blu tack on the ends to trace the shape of the object and stick the sticks to the wall. Place the stick along the side of the object pointing to the wall. Push the stick towards the wall until the blu tack sticks to the wall. The stick should remain in a horizontal position, stuck to the wall.

Once the object is removed, the shape traced by the sticks should be the same. Now put the object back where it was, turn a torch on and shine it at the object, directly in front of it. Turn off the main lights and see if the shadow is the same shape of the outline shown in sticks.

This should establish that the light must be travelling in straight lines like the sticks.

Health and safety

Hazard and risk	Precautions
Kebab sticks have sharp ends and can splinter, causing cuts.	Use under supervision. Cut off the sharp points before giving them to students. Attach a large ball of blu tack to the end of the kebab stick. Discard if damaged.
Blu tack can get into hair or onto clothes, students may be tempted to eat it.	Use non-toxic blu tack from a reputable supplier. Use under supervision. Only hand out blu tack as it is needed.
Torches can be bright and hurt the eyes or even damage eye sight.	Use under supervision, do not shine directly at people.

Adapting the activity
Extra support: reverse the activity, and use the torch to cast a shadow, then trace the shadow in kebab sticks or even white board marker on to a whiteboard.
Extension: shine a torch from the side of the object – what happens to the shadow now? Why? Can you still trace the outline of the object?
Optional extras: revisit and build on learning from Year 3. What happens to the shadow if the torch is moved closer to the object? What happened to the object if the torch is moved further away?

SEEING OBJECTS

Equipment:
A room that can be made dark
The main light in that room

Objects to look at
Light up objects to look at, e.g. battery powered candle

Instructions:
This can be done as groups or as individuals if enough objects are available. Question sheets could be prepared for students to answer after the activity.

1. Place an object in front of the students. Can they see it?
2. Switch the light off in the room so it is dark. Can they see the object now?
3. Ask why the students cannot see the object.
4. With the lights on, swap the object for a light up object such as a battery powered candle. Can they see it?
5. Switch off the light so the room is dark. Can they still see the object? Why?

Establish that they can see the light up object because the light travels from the object to their eyes. Normally, they need light to travel to an object and bounce off it to their eyes.

Health and safety

Hazard and risk	Precautions
Dark rooms – students can trip or fall in the dark, may fear the dark. Some students may be sensitive to changes in brightness.	Lights should be turned back on immediately if students are in distress. The room does not have to be completely dark. Students and staff should not move from their positions in the dark. Check medical needs of students before commencing activity.
Objects and light up objects may fall over and break, fire risk from light up objects.	Use only battery powered light up objects to avoid fire risk. Use small stable objects that do not have to balance so are less likely to fall. Discard damaged objects immediately.

Adapting the activity
Extra support: lead the activity from the front of the room with larger objects.
Extension: try turning away from the light up object. Can they still it? Reinforce the idea that light travels in straight lines.
Optional extras: how can you see your reflection in mirror?

Year 6 Electricity

National Curriculum Statements:

- associate the brightness of a lamp or the volume of a buzzer with the number and voltage of cells used in the circuit;
- compare and give reasons for variations in how components function, including the brightness of bulbs, the loudness of buzzers and the on/off position of switches;
- use recognised symbols when representing a simple circuit in a diagram.

Working scientifically:

- reporting and presenting findings from enquiries, including conclusions, causal relationships and explanations of and a degree of trust in results, in oral and written forms such as displays and other presentations;
- planning different types of scientific enquiries to answer questions, including recognising and controlling variables where necessary.

NC Assessment Indicators

Emerging: recognise circuit symbols.
Expected: construct a series circuit and represent it using circuit symbols.
Exceeding: suggest why the brightness of bulbs change when more are added to a series circuit.

CIRCUIT SYMBOL SNAP

Equipment:
Cards with circuit symbols – bulb, wire, cell, battery, switch, motor, buzzer, etc.
Cards with corresponding written names of symbols
Make sure cards are all the same size and contain repeats to aid memory, e.g. there might be three bulb symbols and bulb word cards in a pack

Instructions:

Introduce the circuit symbols and names to the students, explaining that standard circuit symbols mean that everyone can understand what is in the circuit.

Now hand out packs of circuit symbol cards. There are two games to play.

Game 1 – matching pairs

Shuffle the cards. Lay them out face down on the table.

Take it in turns to turn over any two cards where they are, allowing everyone to see the symbols or names revealed. If they match, pick them up and put them to one side. If they do not match, turn them back over where they are. Now the next person has a turn.

The winner has matched the most pairs!

Game 2 – circuit snap!

Snaps can either be two matching symbols or a symbol with matching written label.

Deal the cards out evenly between the players. The players take turns to turn over one of their cards and place it in the middle. If a card placed down matches the one underneath, then players shout snap and try to be the first to touch the pile. Whoever wins the snap collects the cards. The first one out is the first player to run out of cards.

Adapting the activity

Extra support: keep a help list of symbols with names that students can check if they are not sure they have a matching pair.

Extension: extra symbols can be added, such as voltmeter and ammeter.

Optional extras: play circuit symbol bingo where students select six symbols and draw them on a piece of paper. The teacher then shouts out a component name and the students can tick it off. The first one to tick off their whole grid of six symbols shouts bingo!

SERIES CIRCUITS

Equipment:

Circuit kits containing wires, bulbs, cells or batteries, switches and buzzers

Instructions:

Ask students to build a series circuit with one battery and one bulb.

Add another bulb – what happens to the brightness of the bulbs?

Add a third bulb. What happens now?

Try adding another battery to the circuit. What happens to the brightness of the bulbs now?

Add a third battery and observe what happens.

Students can write a report or answer questions to record their observations. Can they suggest why the brightness of the bulbs changed?

Ask students to build a circuit with a bulb and a buzzer and two batteries. The bulb will light up if the circuit is connected properly. The buzzer will only work if connected the right way around.

Ask students to experiment with the number of batteries in the circuit and record their observations.

Can students conclude why there is a change in loudness of the buzzers?

Now build a circuit with bulbs, buzzers and switches. What happens when the switch/switches are off? Can students explain why?

Health and safety

Hazard and risk	Precautions
Electrical circuit components can cause electric shock.	Use under supervision. Batteries limit the voltage available for electric shock so minimises the risk. Make sure to discuss electrical safely with students before commencing the activity.
Bulbs can break, and broken glass can cause cuts.	Use under supervision and discard if damaged. Glass should be cleared by an adult immediately and disposed of safely.
Sensitivity to light and sound may cause distress in some students.	Be aware of any additional requirements or medical issue of students. Ear protection may be required or a separate space for experimentation.

Adapting the activity
Extra support: assist in the building of circuits or provide simple circuit diagrams for the students to follow.
Extension: work out the voltage for the circuits by adding together the voltage of each battery.
Optional extras: design a circuit for a door bell on a door and draw it using circuit symbols.

Index

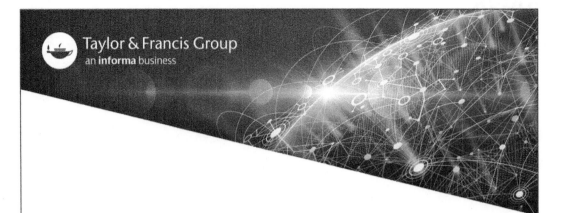